"Being a woman in the spotlight at church [...] your marriage, even your clothes are under th[...] Stephanie, and Jenna get it. They're like your [...] ing you on as you learn to put down the m[...] embrace authenticity (even if it makes tongues wag!), and find delight in serving God again."

Sheila Wray Gregoire, author of *The Great Sex Rescue* and founder of BareMarriage.com

"Stephanie, Jessica, and Jenna beautifully celebrate their roles as pastors' wives while reminding those who share this title that they are unique daughters of God with a story, a calling, and individual personality and style. This is the book I wish my mom could have read as a pastor's wife, and one you will want to share with yours. Grab a tissue to catch your tears of laughter and relief. You aren't alone, dear pastors' wives, and you are so very loved."

Natalie Runion, founder of Raised to Stay and author of the *USA Today* bestseller *Raised to Stay*

"I'm always encouraged by the authenticity that oozes out of Stephanie, Jenna, and Jessica as they capture the hard, the holy, and the hilarious of this important but often unspoken role. Whether you are a pastor's wife or you know a pastor's wife, this book will encourage your soul, direct your prayers, and empower you to love God's church well."

Michelle Myers, cohost of the *She Works His Way* podcast, author, and speaker

"*Pastors' Wives Tell All* is the book every pastor's wife needs to feel seen, understood, and encouraged in a role that is immensely important yet surprisingly isolating and challenging at times. While reading the relatable words and stories from Stephanie, Jenna, and Jessica, pastors' wives will laugh and cry—but more importantly walk away feeling permission to be human, love God, and confidently live the call they have on their own life: to be the unique pastors' wives God has called them to be."

Quinn Kelly, author, speaker, licensed marriage and family therapist, and host of the *Renew You* podcast

"Finally, a book that gets real and relatable about topics the church typically avoids. These pastors' wives are not preaching at you; they are getting deep in the muck with you. This book is a must-read if you want to laugh, cry, and feel empowered to keep chasing Jesus."

Christy Boulware, author of *Nervous Breakthrough* and founder and president of Fearless Unite

"*Pastors' Wives Tell All* is a refreshing breath of honesty and humor that reminds us that even in the holiest of places, life can be wonderfully, delightfully human. This book is a warm hug from women who really believe and live out the truth that God never called us to be superhuman, no matter what our role or title may be. In a world that can often feel isolating and demanding, *Pastors' Wives Tell All* will instantly make you feel as if you're sitting on the couch with your girlfriends and sipping a cup of coffee, all while learning how to live more wisely and love more deeply. What a beautiful ride it is."

Lindsey Maestas, Christian speaker and host
of the *Living Easy with Lindsey* podcast

"*Pastors' Wives Tell All* is a gift to ministry leaders who feel alone and to those in the congregation who could use a behind-the-scenes peek at the real struggles of their leaders. As a former pastor's kid, I am thankful the authors approach this subject authentically yet humorously. I will recommend this resource to ministry leaders from all walks of life in my counseling practice."

Rachael Gilbert, MMFT, owner of BBC Health, author,
and host of *Real Talk with Rachael*

"If you are looking for a book for pastors' wives that's neatly tied in a bow, is void of struggle, and maybe sounds good but is sanitized of real-life experience, THIS IS NOT THAT BOOK. Between these three women, they've seen it all. If you'd consider yourself anything but a stereotypical pastor's wife, this book will encourage you to keep going, remember where your identity lies, and never seek approval from the opinions of well-intentioned church members. God has called you to an important work, and Stephanie, Jenna, and Jessica will help you stay on mission (oh, and laugh a lot)!"

Rebecca George, author of *Do the Thing* and host
of the *Radical Radiance* podcast

"Authentic and hilarious! This is comprehensive encouragement for every aspect of pastor's wife life. Stephanie, Jessica, and Jenna have woven together a book that's as seamless as their Instagram dance routines. If you're married to a man in ministry, this book will help you feel seen and understood in your unique role."

Heather Creekmore, pastor's wife, host of the *Compared to Who?*
podcast, and author of *The 40-Day Body Image Workbook*

"My family has served in pastoral ministry for over twenty years, and I've witnessed how church leadership and ministry can be a lonely, confusing space to navigate. In *Pastors' Wives Tell All*, Stephanie, Jessica, and Jenna open a welcoming door into their hard-won wisdom and winsome stories. These pages offer a field manual of sorts, promising that none of us is really alone and this ministry road not only is possible to navigate but can be a place of growth, freedom, grace, and hope."

Carrie Stephens, author of *Holy Guacamole*
and *Friendship Can Save the World*

PASTORS' WIVES TELL ALL

Navigating Real CHURCH LiFE with Honesty and Humor

STEPHANIE GILBERT, JESSICA TAYLOR, AND JENNA ALLEN

BakerBooks

a division of Baker Publishing Group
Grand Rapids, Michigan

© 2024 by Stephanie Gilbert, Jessica Taylor, and Jenna Allen

Published by Baker Books
a division of Baker Publishing Group
Grand Rapids, Michigan
BakerBooks.com

Printed in the United States of America

Library of Congress Cataloging-in-Publication Data
Names: Gilbert, Stephanie L., 1985– author. | Taylor, Jessica, 1983– author. | Allen,
    Jenna, 1985– author.
Title: Pastors' wives tell all : navigating real church life with honesty and humor /
    Stephanie Gilbert, Jessica Taylor, and Jenna Allen.
Description: Grand Rapids, Michigan : Baker Books, a division of Baker Publishing
    Group, [2024] | Includes bibliographical references.
Identifiers: LCCN 2023036746 | ISBN 9781540903747 (paper) | ISBN 9781540903877
    (casebound) | ISBN 9781493444090 (ebook)
Subjects: LCSH: Spouses of clergy—United States—Religious life. | Christian
    women—United States—Religious life.
Classification: LCC BV4395 .G55 2024 | DDC 253/.22—dc23/eng/20231024
LC record available at https://lccn.loc.gov/2023036746

Unless otherwise indicated, Scripture quotations are from the *Holy Bible*, New Living
Translation. Copyright © 1996, 2004, 2015 by Tyndale House Foundation. Used by permission of Tyndale House Publishers, Carol Stream, Illinois 60188. All rights reserved.

Scripture quotations labeled CSB are from the Christian Standard Bible®. Copyright
© 2017 by Holman Bible Publishers. Used by permission. Christian Standard Bible®
and CSB® are federally registered trademarks of Holman Bible Publishers.

Scripture quotations labeled ESV are from The Holy Bible, English Standard Version®
(ESV®). Copyright © 2001 by Crossway, a publishing ministry of Good News Publishers. Used by permission. All rights reserved. ESV Text Edition: 2016

Scripture quotations labeled KJV are from the King James Version of the Bible.

Scripture quotations labeled NIV are from the Holy Bible, New International Ver-
sion®, NIV®. Copyright © 1973, 1978, 1984, 2011 by Biblica, Inc.® Used by permission
of Zondervan. All rights reserved worldwide. www.zondervan.com. The "NIV" and
"New International Version" are trademarks registered in the United States Patent
and Trademark Office by Biblica, Inc.®

The authors are represented by the literary agency of Mary DeMuth Literary.

Baker Publishing Group publications use paper produced from sustainable forestry
practices and postconsumer waste whenever possible.

24   25   26   27   28   29   30   7   6   5   4   3   2   1

To the pastors who made us pastors' wives:
Isaac Gilbert, Jonathan Taylor, and Ian Allen.

And to the PKs who call us Mom: Bryce, Bentley,
Avery G., Grace, Oliviya, Addie, and Avery A.
You will forever be our first and favorite ministry.

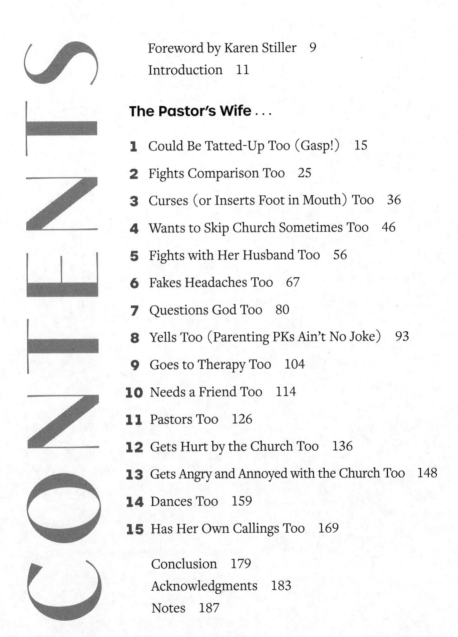

CONTENTS

Foreword

"It's a beautiful and difficult life." That is how I most often describe what life as a pastor's wife is like to those who ask—if I think they can handle the truth. I leave my explanation just that simple, because it's just that complicated.

How do we explain the lovely and the hard? How do we say that absurdity can occasionally stand beside holiness, and that loneliness and way too much company can both be true in the same house and the same heart at the same time?

In church, we have so many jaw-dropping, eye-rolling, and tear-wiping stories of people being their most unusual selves. A lot of those stories we can tell quietly only to each other, because we *get it*. We get each other. We understand the weird.

Church can be so, so good, and church can turn on a dime. We're not surprised, because we know our own flickering, inconsistent hearts. But still, we search for and try to cobuild something true and right and noble, through the grace of God and as we walk beside our beloveds who have this rare calling.

Blessed are the lionhearted pastors' wives, who—yes, a lot of the time—carry the lion's share of home creating and tucking in, Sunday school leading and committee chairing, floor sweeping and fence building, sermon listening and maybe some gentle sermon critiquing much later in the afternoon. All of this while trying to love those pastor husbands of ours so well, the ones who work so hard that we must remind them we are also their people, and we need them too.

"Come home soon," we might have to say, or "I'm driving down to get you."

Some days this pastor-wife life can feel heavy. On just such a day a few years ago, I came upon three pastors' wives on Instagram laughing with joy, being a bit loud, teasing each other, and dancing in a way that made me laugh and shake my head. They were so silly and fun, but Stephanie, Jenna, and Jessica were also speaking out loud what most others only whisper about being a pastor's wife.

They were so honest. I loved them instantly. You will too.

Pastors' Wives Tell All is a "how-to" book, but it's also a "why" book that reminds us that this life is special and sacred, and that there is joy. There is advice to be had here on sex, therapy, parenting, clothing, rest, and so much more. Like a good friend would give. "When Grownups Act Like Toddlers," is a heading in this book, and that should tell you everything you need to know about the light and the weight and depth of what you are about to read.

If you've longed for friends who can listen and laugh, and to whom you could say anything and it would be just fine, then be welcome here, strong friend. We need each other. Here is a room filled with light where we can find each other.

Karen Stiller, author of *The Minister's Wife: A Memoir of Faith,
Doubt, Friendship, Loneliness, Forgiveness, and More*
and *Holiness Here: Searching for God in the Ordinary
Events of Everyday Life*; KarenStiller.com

Introduction

They say getting a tattoo is addictive. Once you've felt the sting of that needle and experienced the pure ecstasy of seeing your body transform into a literal piece of art before your eyes, there's no going back—literally, of course, because what's done is, most assuredly, positively d-o-n-e *done*. But there's also a realization that there is no going back to the person you were before this monumental change. You've officially joined the club, the unofficial tatted-up club. (We're sure there's a T-shirt for that somewhere.) You have stepped into a new phase of life. One where you are simultaneously unafraid of change *and* dedicated to permanence, as you have just experienced one of the most permanent changes of your life. It's a beautiful juxtaposition of sorts.

This is what being a pastor's wife is like—a permanent change in your life that marks you. It leaves a lasting impression, whether completely awkward like a tattoo chosen in an impulsive stupor, or gloriously meaningful like a tattoo that's been wrestled with and prayed over for years before taking the plunge.

Once you've witnessed church and ministry life behind the scenes, there's no unseeing it. Let's get real. Church people are messy. Pastors' wives are messy. Every person who has ever served the church in any capacity is messy. We are all imperfect, hard to get along with at times, stubborn, and selfish. It's the sad reality of being flawed human beings. Don't believe us? If you are void of all imperfection, you might want to stop here and pack it up, sister, because this book ain't for you (excuse our grammar).

The three of us—Jenna, Jessica, and Stephanie—are women who have been marked in the deepest of ways by the title "pastor's wife." We know what it's like to walk alongside church people as they step into a new marriage, choose a college to attend, grieve the loss of a loved one, or experience a painful divorce. We journey with them as they make life-altering decisions like choosing to follow Jesus or changing their hairstyle (don't act like you've never seen a hairstyle change a life before) and everything in between. We've been chewed out by our critics about as hard as we've been bear-hugged by those who truly see and appreciate us. We've been used, abused, loved, honored, held, and discarded more times than we can count. And along the way, we've learned a thing or two.

This book is for the pastor's wife, the female pastor, the lady leading a ministry, and the female church member who has been helped (or hindered) by her church leaders and truly wants to understand why church leadership makes the decisions it does.

> The ministry leader who has been gutted by the people she desperately wishes to serve and be loved by.
>
> The pastor's wife who feels like a single mom because her husband spends every waking moment counseling, responding to emergency phone calls, studying for sermons, and taking on one more thing because the concept of boundaries is just out of reach.

The church leader who collapses after a week of late nights
and proceeds to shovel popcorn by the fistful into her
mouth while catching up on *Friends* and *Vampire Diaries*
reruns.

The woman who, below her polished, smiling surface,
resents her husband for choosing "ministry" over her
and their family.

The leader who is surrounded by people almost daily yet
feels utterly alone.

The pastor's wife who has grieved the loss of friendships
and struggles to find the kind of friendships that stick,
real ones where she can be her *real* self . . . because it's
totally "in" to be authentic, transparent, and vulnerable—
unless you're the pastor's wife.

If you can relate to any of these scenarios, then, friend, you've
come to the right place. You've cracked open the exact right
book. You are our kind of people.

————

We don't know about you, but we're tired of hiding in the
shadows, of being a mystery to our church families and being
placed on unreachable pedestals. It's about time we kicked the
pedestals out from under ourselves, because some of us could
use a bruised behind. We are no better than any of the women
beside us in the pews and certainly have not "arrived."

We strive for holiness even though our jeans are the only
"holey" thing about us some days. Our marriages have suffered.
Our parenting has been marked by impatience and even selfish-
ness. Our homes have found themselves in utter disarray. And
we may have even lost our cool a time or two with the people
we are supposed to love and serve. Yes, we sin. And sure, we

are never meant to remain in sin. But that's true for *all* Jesus followers, not just ministers and spouses.

And as we navigate a life surrendered to God's leading, we discover the greatest journey of our lives—a journey that is both brimming with heartache and bubbling over with joy. If you haven't gotten to the joy part yet, hold on to your leggings, girlfriend, because we are about to go for a ride where the destination is a life of ministry marked by hope, even when critics and grief abound. We'll find the path to the kind of ministry that is more like the deliberate, prayed-over tattoo that serves as a permanent reminder of the grace and hope we've found in our Jesus.

Speaking of tats . . .

1

~~~~~~

The Pastor's Wife
Could Be Tatted-Up Too (Gasp!)

> To be yourself in a world that is constantly trying to make you
> something else is the greatest accomplishment.
>
> —Ralph Waldo Emerson

The three of us have matching tattoos. Yes, sirree, we do. But
before we took the plunge into permanent ink, we did what
any intelligent millennials would do: we polled Instagram to
help us decide between two ideas we were juggling, and like
any good millennial who polls Instagram followers, we went
with . . . neither. Our finickiness did not deter our social media
friends from offering tons of great suggestions, however. And
as the creative and sentimental tattoo ideas began flowing from
our Instagram friends, so did the criticism.

"Why would you mark your bodies when God is against it?"

"Shouldn't you be a better example for the people following you?"

Meet Mrs. PPPW

When you are a pastor's wife, people have numerous opinions about what you should look like. *Lots.* And many of those opinions have no scriptural backing. But don't most of us already have a preconceived picture of the ideal pastor's wife? Picture with us Mrs. Perky Perfect Pastor's Wife. Let's call her Mrs. PPPW for short. Mrs. PPPW is the very definition of that good ole churchy word, *modest*, while still appearing somewhat (but not too) trendy. Without a hint of unkempt hair, she's neatly styled and pulled together with her trendy-not-trendy dress flowing down just below her kneecaps (because knees are sexy and should *never* be exposed). Mrs. PPPW quietly accepts demands from her husband and the church while serving with a smile in her meek-and-quiet-spirit way. She's a pure gem.

So, what happens when you marry a pastor yet you fall two sexy-showing kneecaps short of the role? (Confession time. It's *us.* We're the ones with the scandalous kneecaps.)

The three of us have come to terms with the fact that we don't fit into the stereotypical pastor's wife mold, and we are perfectly fine with being quirky. Yes, we have tattoos. Yes, we dye our hair. We wear jeans with holes in them (even on Sundays). Of course, none of these outward traits encompass us entirely. God didn't place us in church ministry because we embody the ideal Mrs. PPPW, and we sure aren't flying our angel wings around on a higher spiritual plane. He called us because He prefers to use cracked and broken vessels with potential over vessels that have sat on a shelf collecting metaphorical dust for the extent of their existence—too perfect to be touched by the observers who stand in awe of their extraordinarily impeccable outsides.

A first-class vessel is great in theory, but what's the point if it never gets used? Sure, the vessels with cracks need sprucing up. But those cracks provide space for the light of Jesus to shine through, while the unblemished version is far too solid to emit even the slightest glimmer. Cracks expose the light, and it is then, when our trials become blatantly obvious, that the people around us find Jesus. If their eyes were too distracted by our fancy, flawless design, they might miss Him. This is the very meaning of a freeing verse in John's Gospel: "He must become greater and greater, and I must become less and less" (3:30). We decrease. He increases. He doesn't need us and our got-it-all-togetherness. He *wants* us, quirks and all.

Don't get us wrong. Sinful actions should be exposed and extracted from our hearts and lives through obedience to our Savior. But that's not what we're talking about here. Some of us have been told we're too loud, too quiet, too mundane, too much, too not enough, too (fill in the blank). For so long we've believed the lie that our personality and sense of style are mistakes. Surely God didn't mean for us to come out quite this, er, "different."

What we forget is that our God is an artist. His creativity is evident in the way He uniquely designed each of us. You might be a dynamic leader who stands out in bold wardrobe options with sassy hair and makeup. Or maybe you're into dark emo hair and pink tips, with jet black as the only shade on your outfit color wheel, and let's not forget that tatted-up sleeve adorning your entire arm. Or perhaps you love dresses and pearls and play the piano with grace and ease. If those style choices reflect who you indeed are, then rock them. No single pastor's wife mold exists.

The Proverbial Fishbowl

For those of you who can't relate because you are wholeheart-edly comfortable in your skin, we applaud you. You know who you are and never shy away from expressing the real you. But it's possible that even with all your confidence, you're still fear-ful of people responding negatively to your style choices. We understand the hesitation. We live in a proverbial fishbowl, but at the same time, people may not be judging us as harshly as we judge ourselves.

Jenna learned this several years ago when she made the "wild" decision to get a nose ring. (Yep, tats aren't the only strike against us.) As she eased her way through the congregation for the first time after that fateful hole-in-her-nose day, fear crept into her heart and insecurity infiltrated her mind. She'd imag-ined all the comments and side-eye stares that would inevitably come from the more "spiritual ones" and had braced herself for them. Surely those more seasoned ladies would have a thing or two to say about her apparent pre-midlife crisis, which caused her to have this moment of "holey" weakness. But as quickly as the fearful anticipation had built, it deflated. The comments never came. The awkward stares were only in her head. Nobody thought less of her; or if they did, they kept it to themselves.

Isn't this how we live too often, expecting the other shoe to drop, so to speak, when we change our outward appearance? How can we expect anyone else to drop the stereotypes if we can't nix them ourselves? If we place weighty expectations on our appearance, consciously or subconsciously, we shouldn't hope for anything different from our church family.

Think about the Scripture passage recounting the day the prophet Samuel anointed the boy who would be the next king of Israel. If Samuel had his way, he would have anointed Jesse's first son, Eliab, and called it a day. Eliab was an obvious choice from the outside, but our God loves to do things backward. He looks from the inside out. And why would we think it'd be any other way? He tells us to *die* (to ourselves) to *live*, after all. It doesn't get more backward than that. God had a different plan than Samuel did for Israel's next leader.

> But the LORD said to Samuel, "Don't judge by his appearance or height, for I have rejected him. The LORD doesn't see things the way you see them. People judge by outward appearance, but the LORD looks at the heart." (1 Sam. 16:7)

And we all know who God chose for this high position of honor and leadership: the smelly, dirty shepherd boy named David. God is not as focused on our appearance as we think He is.

Legalism Is the Enemy

Stephanie remembers well growing up in a church culture that thrived on sermons that condemned a plethora of hair and clothing styles. If you were a woman with a short pixie cut or a man with long locks, you must be a follower of Satan himself. Wearing shorts in the summertime—what could have possibly possessed you? It couldn't be the Holy Spirit. Sadly, we're not joking. This church prioritized cleaning up the outside before they addressed the inside. Legalism was a friend to them. But the inside matters most, not our human rules and regulations about how we dress on the outside. You can be the most trendy, modest, cleaned-up Christian woman on the outside and be nothing but a rotting corpse on the inside . . . utterly spiritually dead, like the religious leaders in Matthew:

> What sorrow awaits you teachers of religious law and you Pharisees. Hypocrites! For you are like whitewashed tombs—

beautiful on the outside but filled on the inside with dead people's bones and all sorts of impurity. (23:27)

There is a reason it seems like our Westernized churches are filled with members *playing* church instead of truly living out the gospel.

Stephanie will always remember a lesson her friend Brittney unwittingly taught her. One Sunday morning, as Brittney scurried around her home, wrangling three children toward the door and into the car to head to church, her daughter's frustration halted her efforts. Whining escalated into a mini meltdown over what to wear to church. This perceptive little girl had noticed that the other girls her age wore adorable smocked frocks to church (you aren't Southern unless you embrace all the "ocks"). She was in a tizzy over what her friends would think about her not-so-ocked dress and did not look forward to making a church appearance without an outfit as cute as theirs.

Brittney knew church outfits were not at the top of Jesus's priority list, so she immediately changed her own clothes. She tore off her dressy ensemble, pulled on a simple pair of jeans and a T-shirt, and told her daughter to do the same. She ignored all the makeup and threw her hair back into a ponytail. She then bent down, peered into her daughter's eyes, and spoke words of truth to her: what we look like on the outside is *not* what's important. What matters is a heart of worship, focusing on the object of worship, Jesus. God isn't impressed with our outward displays of righteousness. He is concerned with our heart's posture. Period. Stephanie's sweet friend recognized this truth and exemplified it through her actions. We can do the same in the ministry God has given us.

Why Moderation Is the Key

Like an onion, this conversation on outward appearance has layers. We understand that in everything there should be a balance. Just because our outward appearance is not our focus does not mean we should flaunt our freedom. The Bible is clear: "For you have been called to live in freedom, my brothers and sisters. But don't use your freedom to satisfy your sinful nature. Instead, use your freedom to serve one another in love" (Gal. 5:13).

Jessica runs a nonprofit called Come Away Missions that serves the people of Rwanda. Each time she flies overseas to spend time with these people she packs different clothes than she would for travel stateside. Yes, Jessica is fiery and loves a comfy pair of leggings or cute jeans with holes in the knees, but she also knows that Rwandan culture is very different from the culture of South Alabama. So, she alters her outward appearance accordingly, setting aside her graphic T-shirts and holey jeans for flowing skirts with splashes of bright color to honor the culture of the Rwandan people. Humility is key.

We are who we are, and we want our personalities to be reflected on the outside. But we can be who we are while still honoring a few preferences of differing cultures. If you serve people in a lower-income neighborhood than your own, dressing in designer high heels and fancy pantsuits may not be the best choice for a Sunday service. Likewise, if you serve in a church where every woman in the congregation wears dresses to services, leggings aren't a viable option. Moderation, moderation, moderation in everything.

"You be you, Boo" has become our modern-day war cry. But if we go too far down the rabbit hole of that mantra, we might forget the command to die to ourselves. It's a tricky balance! Yes, display the real you. Wear what fits the personality God gave you. Get the cute tattoo. But keep it humble, because pride will erode ministries like cancer. Don't be the church leader who likes to make a point rather than make disciples of Jesus Christ.

Ultimately, our identity is not tied to how we present ourselves on the outside. The inside will eventually outshine all our veneers. And if we have been made new in Christ, *He* is our identity. We have the head knowledge of this truth, but sometimes we need more heart knowledge.

If your heart has forgotten, let's take a trip down Scripture lane, shall we?

> My old self has been crucified with Christ. It is no longer I who live, but Christ lives in me. So I live in this earthly body by trusting in the Son of God, who loved me and gave himself for me. (Gal. 2:20)

> For we are God's masterpiece. He has created us anew in Christ Jesus, so we can do the good things he planned for us long ago. (Eph. 2:10)

> Thank you for making me so wonderfully complex!
> Your workmanship is marvelous—how well I know it.
> (Ps. 139:14)

Our Father created us, died for us, saved us, and sustains us. He is everything we need and always will be.

When Christ is our identity, everything else falls away: the pressure to live up to a false narrative of what a pastor's wife should look like; the suffocating, legalistic guidelines tradition has placed upon us; the lie that our personalities should be under lock and key so as to not draw too much attention to ourselves; the fear of our outward appearance not being good enough for our church people. It's not all about us. In every possible way, it is all about Him. Christ is enough, and He is making us enough.

The Narcissistic Pastor's Wife

As podcasters and pastors' wives, we've heard our fair share of strange stories *from* pastors' wives and *about* pastors' wives. One story a friend on social media shared about her pastor's wife had us bowing our heads in vicarious embarrassment. This pastor's wife had an assistant who stuck to her side on Sundays, keeping her water bottle filled and tissues on hand. And when it came time for the service to begin, the pastor's wife positioned herself on the platform for everyone to see, her attitude and actions totally out of sync with the church's culture. In her eyes, being a pastor's wife equaled royalty.

Narcissism is an epidemic that has run rampant among clergy for years. We don't like to admit it, but it's true. Church hurt, spiritual abuse, and other destructive fruits of narcissism aren't just buzzwords we toss around on social media (and we will talk about that in a later chapter). They are a virus attacking the church from every direction, and pastors' wives aren't immune to the destruction.

We need to check our hearts. Let's not be the ones whose actions shout, "I don't care what you think. I'll wear what I want to wear, do what I want to do, and pierce what I want to pierce, and you can't do a thing about it!" Instead, we can consider the culture of the community God has called us to serve and stay humble in our decisions.

We know it's unhealthy for a church to dictate what a pastor's wife should wear. That should be a decision she and her husband make in the privacy of their own home. But we can choose to open our eyes to our church's atmosphere and be humble enough to make respectful choices. Balance is key. Our outward appearance should never be our primary concern. Our willingness to learn, seek humility, and love our neighbors well is what matters in the long run.

To sum it all up: Love God. Love people. Get the tattoo.

2

The Pastor's Wife
Fights Comparison Too

We won't be distracted by comparison if we are captivated with purpose.

—Bob Goff

We all have an inner middle schooler attempting to claw her way to the surface. An insecure, acne-prone, damaged tween who can muster up zero positive things to say about herself. Bless her heart. We feed her insecurities, indulge her pitiful *woe is me* thoughts, and even convince her that it is still acceptable to feel this way—entirely typical.

This is how comparison works. She disguises herself as a natural part of life we all face, like the insecurities that attack every preteen. But this is how she deceives and, ultimately, entraps us. The truth is, we don't have to be suckered into believing this lie. We don't have to feed the insecurities of our inner tween. Comparison has no right to dig her devious claws into our daily thoughts. We can be free from her grasp and consciously safeguard our minds from her lies, just as a middle schooler can be set free from insecurity.

The Ultimate Frenemy

Although comparison can affect all women, she becomes explicitly crafty when influencing church leaders. Remember our good ole frenemy, Mrs. PPPW? She is perfection incarnate. She strokes those piano keys with elegance, never raises her voice, keeps calm under insurmountable pressure, and loves people so well that everyone who crosses her path feels eternally changed for the better. (Panic attack, anyone?) This is the picture of perfection many of us compare ourselves to when stepping into church leadership roles. We beat ourselves up for never meeting these extraordinary—and entirely imaginary—requirements.

It doesn't help when church people assume we are the blessed PPPW: "You must never struggle with X, Y, or Z, huh? I wish I had the type of relationship with God you must have. If only I could be as solid and spiritual as you are."

Do such statements make anybody else want to barf right about now? Between our imaginations and church people's expectations, it's no wonder we fall prey to comparison. When our church family assumes we are more spiritual than they are, we get stuck comparing ourselves to the fantasy pastor's wife the church has concocted.

Being compared to Mrs. PPPW isn't the only way comparison appears in the church. It gets stickier when the pastor's wife is compared to an *actual* former pastor's wife. This pressure cooker of a situation does no one any good. High expectations take on a monstrous new form, because this type of comparison is based on the reality that there is a pastor's wife who is adored more than we are.

When You Can't Live Up to Her

Before Jessica and her husband, Jonathan, took over the pastorate at their church, they interned at their new church home while the former pastor still served there. Jessica remembers how deeply the church people loved their pastor's wife. And who wouldn't adore her? She poured her heart and soul into the children's ministry. She was a listening ear and a shoulder to cry on for the women in the church. She unified the church staff effortlessly and led with dignity and grace. Jessica couldn't help but admire her. But admiration morphed into something different as the time came for her and her husband to step into the pastoral role. Comparison gnawed glaring holes into her confidence in her calling from God.

She found herself believing a whole string of lies and unhelpful questions.

I'm not as old as she is, so people won't respect me as they respect her.

I do not want to run the children's ministry, but she does it well. How can I live up to that?

She has built such strong bonds; they planted this church. What if I never experience those bonds too?

Will they ever love me as much as they love her?

Jessica's experience with past church hurt did her no favors either. Trust is difficult when a church has deeply wounded you, and believing you can be both vulnerable and loved becomes an unreachable fantasy. This lethal combination also creates a ripe breeding ground for comparison.

27

Ultimately, comparison is jealousy, and jealousy within a church staff should be swiftly squashed. James speaks candidly on this matter: "For wherever there is jealousy and selfish ambition, there you will find disorder and evil of every kind" (3:16). Because of God's Word, the Holy Spirit, and her fierce competitive side, Jessica would not allow comparison a win. She fought until she found peace in not being exactly like the former pastor's wife. And by golly, she didn't need to be. She could rejoice over this woman's talents without the sting of jealousy. God called that pastor's wife to serve within the specific giftings God had bestowed on her, and God called Jessica to serve within her own gifts. Both brought value to the table. Neither trumped the other. That inner, insecure middle schooler could be put to rest once and for all. (And angels sang triumphantly in the background.)

Often we are our worst enemy regarding comparison, but sometimes well-meaning (and not-so-well-meaning) churchgoers do the job for us. Little jabs and unwelcome reminders come rolling off the tongue a bit too easily for them:

"Our previous pastor's wife always worked in the nursery without complaint."

"Our other pastor's wife sang in the choir and served on the worship team. What can you do?"

"We sure loved when our former pastor's wife ran the women's ministry and led Bible study every week."

"Angels would descend like doves upon our pastor's wife's crown each time she glided across the sanctuary threshold! You should have seen the sparks that flew when she breathed her sweet angel breath across the leather spine of her family King James Bible."

Okay, so maybe that last one is a bit of an exaggeration, but that's just about how it feels to the pastor's wife receiving such comparisons. Some people don't understand what their words can stir up in us, and others know *exactly* what they are doing. Either way, it's not healthy to internalize these comparisons. God isn't expecting you to suddenly become a piano-playing whiz when you've never touched a single key in your entire life. He's not surprised by your quiet demeanor or your center stage personality. As you walk out your calling in service to the church, and ultimately to the Lord, He sees you as enough—not "sort of okay" enough, or "that'll do" enough, but simply *enough*.

And, church, we want you to know that we love and appreciate your sweet and thoughtful words. We do. But please, stop assuming we don't struggle as you do. You're either sending your leaders into a tailspin of comparison *or* feeding their sinful pride. Either way, it's a lose-lose situation. Your words have more power than you realize.

The Trouble with Talented Friends

Comparison is a sneaky little booger. It pops up where we least expect it. Friendship is one of these cunning places. None of us would say that we don't want our friends to be successful. Of course we do! Who doesn't want to cheer on their best friend as she slays her calling, discovers new and exciting opportunities, or chooses a rocking new outfit (priorities, you know)? But amid all the joy we feel for our friends, sometimes comparison likes to show up to the party uninvited.

Jenna has been there. The nerves hit hard when we led our first overnight pastors' wives retreat—teaching women who might have more knowledge and experience than you is intimidating as it is. But when you don't feel that speaking and teaching are your gifts, that packs on even more unwanted pressure. Jenna compared her teaching skill to Stephanie's and Jessica's, even though none of us teach the same way. But that's honestly what makes our team work so well. In a moment of insecurity, as we climbed into bed in the wee hours of the morning that first retreat night, Jenna collapsed into tears.

The enemy knows exactly how to attack, and he does it well. Jenna is a team player and a cheerleader for her friends. She would never begrudge any of them their giftings, but her self-criticism cracked the door open for comparison to slip in. However, the enemy didn't know what hit him after he'd interfered with our friend. A pep talk, prayer, and truth bombs followed, and she proverbially sucker punched comparison right in its face. (And yes, we said "sucker punched." It felt right.) Jenna brought her defeating thoughts to the light by sharing them with us. We prayed together and spoke the truth out loud. The enemy loses power when we embrace God's truth and bring our hidden thoughts and fears to the light.

Jenna went even further by sharing her insecurity with the small group she led that weekend. As she let down her guard, other women began doing the same. Women found freedom from their hidden insecurities all because Jenna found the courage to share her own.

We can honor our fellow PW (pastor's wife) friends' strengths while allowing God to use us in our weaknesses. Let's stay in our lane, as Galatians teaches: "Pay careful attention to your own work, for then you will get the satisfaction of a job well done, and you won't need to compare yourself to anyone else. For we are each responsible for our own conduct" (6:4–5).

The Husband-Wife Bench of Comparison

You might not be comparing yourself to friends or even other pastors' wives. Perhaps what you fret over is whether you are as good at ministry things as your husband. There is already so much opportunity for spouses to compete as it is. Who does the heaviest lifting for the family? Who is the most selfless? Who makes the most money? Who does the best housework? Who is the favorite parent? (The answer to that one is always Mom.) We're supposed to be a team, yet comparison can sneak in and erode our marital foundation with stealth and ease. Pastoral marriages are no exception. We've seen it happen, whether it's the pastor's wife attempting to speak with as much skill as her husband, or the pastor getting frustrated when his wife's creative outreach ideas work better than his. No one is safe from moments of comparison.

If comparison can't win any other way, it will poke and prod that marital foundation. Allow us to free you right quick. You are *not* your husband. (Shocking, we know. You can pick your jaw up off the floor now.) You are not expected to do everything your husband does or be all the things he is. You can be fully you, serving in your capacity. Stop lingering on the sidelines trying to be someone different. Sitting on the bench of comparison isn't a good look on you. Get in the game with *your* giftings.

Stephanie and her husband, Isaac, served for over a decade at their first church, which is in a quaint Alabama town of just over two thousand people where neighbors can borrow a cup of sugar from each other and family roots run deep. Isaac began serving there a year before they were married, which gave him time to connect with the people. As a good ole country boy, he fit in quite nicely with the small-town Southern life. On the other hand, Stephanie grew up near Tampa, Florida, which has no shortage of crowds, hustle and bustle, and cultural diversity. So, as you can imagine, getting married and immediately moving to a town with two stoplights was quite a culture shock for her.

As she attempted to settle into her new home, Stephanie could see how dearly the community and church loved her husband. She appreciated how well the people accepted him and looked forward to adapting to ministry life as quickly as Isaac. The first few years weren't bad—many great memories were made—but as time passed, she began to feel as though people didn't love and accept her as much as they loved and accepted her youth pastor husband. The more she tried to relate to the other women in her church, the more she felt like the odd person out. Isaac was thriving there, so why couldn't she? Comparison whispered in her ear nearly daily as her husband found joy in his workspace. Over time, she grew tired of striving to belong and hit her personal rock bottom.

Comparing herself to her husband sent her on a downward spiral. As she placed more expectations on herself to fit in and be noticed like Isaac, she grew sadder and more unfulfilled. Misery became a close comrade. Even though she was an extrovert and flourished off other people's energy, she began secluding herself and wasted too many hours in tears.

It took a combination of self-work, prayer, and time for Stephanie to become confident in the person God created her to be. She could let her husband be the country boy he was while she rocked her city-loving self, even if it meant being the only city girl in the room. Her anxiety lifted as she rested in the truth: "For God has not given us a spirit of fear and timidity, but of power, love, and self-discipline" (2 Tim. 1:7). God-confidence filled her, and comparison retreated.

When You Become the Problem

Now, what if you are on the opposite end of the spectrum? You notice another woman in ministry who isn't doing nearly as much as you. Sure, she serves in her own cute, small-scale capacity, but you have some *extraordinary* gifts you're using. Or maybe you're hard on yourself, but you soothe your wounded ego by comparing what you do to that woman who is serving differently. Inadvertently, you place expectations on your fellow pastor's wife, becoming comparison's vehicle. You cause her to stumble into her own head-on collision with comparison, totaling all confidence she should have in Christ's calling.

When we become the problem, pride evolves into a near and dear friend as we elevate ourselves according to the warped standard we've created. God's Word expresses His disdain for such selfish pride: "Don't be selfish; don't try to impress others. Be humble, thinking of others as better than yourselves" (Phil. 2:3). The Bible also clearly teaches us how absurd comparing others to ourselves is:

> Oh, don't worry; we wouldn't dare say that we are as wonderful as these other men who tell you how important they are! But they are only comparing themselves with each other, using themselves as the standard of measurement. How ignorant! (2 Cor. 10:12)

Friend, we want better for you. God wants better for you. You can catch the signs of comparison before it takes root. But before any of us can recognize the symptoms, we must grasp the underlying problem with comparison.

The Disco Ball Effect

We notice bright and shiny things—like the disco ball lighting up the high school dance as we jammed to Boyz II Men like it was 1999 . . . and, also, it *was* 1999. But you get the point. Shiny things make us happy. So, it should be no surprise when we notice bright and shining people—the ones who seem to live extraordinary lives, accomplishing every goal they strive to reach. Seeing these individuals isn't the problem. The downfall comes when those bright and shiny people start affecting our identity. When we put ourselves down or build up our selfish pride by comparing, we have forgotten who we are in Christ. Christ is not enough for us.

The real question is, Who are we trying to please? Other people? Ourselves? God? It can't be all three; only one will lead to success. People may never love you as much as they love *her*. They may not even love you as much as they love your husband. But ultimately, their approval is trivial. We will never be free from comparison's tight grasp until we understand whose approval really matters: "Obviously, I'm not trying to win the approval of people, but of God. If pleasing people were my goal, I would not be Christ's servant" (Gal. 1:10). If we are Christ's servants, we should live to please only Him.

Set aside time for self-reflection and answer these questions honestly:

Am I attempting to build relationships with my church family, or am I trying to perform to impress them?
Am I walking in the Spirit, or am I walking in the flesh?

Instead of measuring your worth and identity in people, use God's gauge: "You are jealous of one another and quarrel with each other. Doesn't that prove you are controlled by your sinful nature? Aren't you living like people of the world?" (1 Cor. 3:3). This behavior comes from the old "man" (or woman) we were without Christ.

It's natural to compare, feel jealous, and act out of our envy, but we were *called out* of our natural selves into our spiritual selves. We are new creations in Christ who can walk in freedom and hope as we serve our churches and communities. Will we embrace our spiritual selves, which are gloriously saved and made new in Christ, or will we wallow in our natural, comparison-wrought old selves?

The three of us are done pitying our insecurity-wrought inner middle schooler. Are you?

3

The Pastor's Wife
Curses (or Inserts Foot in Mouth) Too

If you think I talk too much, let me know. We can talk about it.

—Anonymous

One or more of us (we won't say who, exactly) was quite the Chatty Cathy as a child. Think of a current-day adult who speaks now, thinks later, and word-vomits their feelings on vaccinations, politics, and breast milk *all* over the social networks. You know the kind. Yes, one of us didn't quite understand why "we" didn't have too many friends to push us on the swings or spin us on that death trap called a merry-go-round on the school playground or braid our golden locks—you get the point. The mouth was trouble, to put it plainly. And to be honest, that trait may have evolved over the years, but it still gets us into all sorts of trouble we could and maybe *should* avoid.

Being a pastor's wife would be about a million times easier if we weren't so human. Wouldn't it be nice if, when you became a pastor, pastor's wife, or any ministry leader, suddenly all your humanness fell away, like a snake shedding its old, crusty skin? Yes, the picture of aging skin falling *far* away from us as we step into our new, glamorous role as pastor's wife is what we'd all love to imagine. (Cue the heavens opening as a majestic band descends, erupting into the most spiritually epic "Hallelujah" chorus *ever*.) But alas, we still must work through our imperfections one day at a time.

The "Mean Girl" Pastor's Wife

The early ministry years are fun, aren't they? You want to believe you have all the answers when there is still so much you don't know. According to Google (which does have all the answers . . . the right *and* the wrong ones, that is), parts of our brains don't reach full development until we're twenty-five.[1] *Twenty-five.* Those of us who have been in ministry since our early twenties feel bad for the people in our churches who had to deal with our lack of brain maturity in those days. Jessica learned a ton about the trouble our mouths can get us into in her early twenties. She might not have been cussing like a sailor (at least not out loud), but she sure spoke the truth with a lot of vigor, to put it nicely.

Let's be honest. When you are positioned in church leadership with an adolescent brain, it's easy to think it's your sacred duty to distribute your God-bestowed wisdom by whatever method best gets the point across, even if it resembles a bulldozer gone haywire in a shoebox apartment directly above the local china shop. Jessica would speak the truth, but she was brazenly harsh and not always considerate of people's feelings. She learned the hard way that you could say all the right things, but if you say them in the wrong ways, you end up pushing people away rather than helping them change for the better. As Proverbs tells us, the tongue is powerful: "The tongue can bring death or life; those who love to talk will reap the consequences" (18:21). We've said it before, and we'll repeat it: too many leaders use their proverbial and literal pulpits to make a point rather than point people to Jesus.

We all need accountability. If it weren't for wise counsel from older, godly leaders, Jessica's mouth could have caused loads of damage to both teenagers and parents alike in those early youth ministry days. Thankfully, she had iron-sharpens-iron friends who knew how to dish the truth back at her, helping to mold and shape her into the leader she is today. She became teachable, as we all should be. "In the same way, you who are younger must accept the authority of the elders. And all of you, dress yourselves in humility as you relate to one another, for 'God opposes the proud but gives grace to the humble'" (1 Pet. 5:5). The mouth that got Jessica into trouble back in the day is the same mouth speaking life over men and women today from a pulpit and a podcast mic.

She still doesn't always get it right. Even with a fully developed adult-ish brain in her, she has made mistakes. Once, memorably, at a church league volleyball game. We all know that church league sports have a way of squashing the holy in people. Just ask Stephanie's husband, who, one week before his wife gave birth to their second child, fractured his elbow and tore his ACL and meniscus completely to shreds (picture a Twizzler gone wrong) because of an opposing player's momentary loss of "the holy." But that's a story for another day.

In such a momentary loss of all things holy and sane, Jessica railed at the line judge across the gym for his apparent lack of sight and knowledge of the game. Regina George from *Mean Girls* would have blushed at this demonstration of mean-girl superiority. Stands full of church members, children (including her own), and other onlookers gawked as her screams echoed across the court. Her team members cringed, and her husband would have crawled into a hole right then and there, never to return, had the opportunity presented itself. And to make matters worse, the arguing persisted for an awkwardly long time. She let him have it amid the crowd of church people, pastor-husband, and God Himself. It wasn't her finest moment.

Before the rest of us get all judgy, let's not pretend we've never let our anger get the best of us. It happens. Once again, that crusty ole humanness latches onto us like soaking-wet jeans on a hot summer day. But we can be thankful for grace and the ability to see what we've done, and course correct. Jessica peeled those proverbial soaking-wet jeans off, threw on a good pair of leggings meant for elder-millennial style and comfort (did we mention their ridiculous comfort?), and made a large round of apologies. She couldn't take back what she'd said, but she could humble herself enough to see how her mouth had gotten the best of her and attempt to make it right.

This is how church ministry life works much of the time. We pray for wisdom as we proclaim the truth of God's Word boldly, but we fail and falter, and, yes, even curse under our breath (and sometimes out loud) when we stub our big toe. The key to a successful ministry is not to never make mistakes or say the wrong thing but to recognize when our tongues have led us astray and own up to it. The book of Proverbs assures us we will fail if we don't: "People who conceal their sins will not prosper, but if they confess and turn from them, they will receive mercy" (28:13).

Spilling the Tea in Prayer Group

Let's take a moment to segue into a much-needed conversation about the elephant in the room. You know, the elephant disguised as a heartfelt prayer request for that "sister in Christ" we're super concerned about because we can't believe who she spent time with or what she did last weekend. "Wait, you mean you haven't heard? Let me fill you in so you can 'pray' for her, because God knows she needs it. How in the world she's done this to herself, I'll never understand." (Insert a highly detailed and grossly specific piece of juicy gossip here.)

We've all been there—the prayer night turned into a gossip-filled nightmare. News flash: church leaders are not immune to gossip, whether we are its topic or its source. We don't ever want to believe we're the problem or the ones stirring up conversations better left unsaid, but it happens, sometimes unintentionally.

We are the keepers of secrets. This is the nature of church leadership. People confide in us with their baggage, struggles, and sins. We are supposed to be a safe space, but sadly, some of us are the furthest thing from "safe." Whether it's spilling someone else's closeted skeletons into the laps of our fellow church staff members, using them in a future sermon, or sharing them during a personal conversation with another church member, some leaders perpetuate the problem of gossip in the church. They sneak and slither like an infestation of snakes, hissing with pointed tongues and preparing their venomous bite. Like Jesus said in the Gospel of Matthew, "You brood of snakes! How could evil men like you speak what is good and right? For whatever is in your heart determines what you say" (12:34). What's in our hearts will come rushing out, and the results can be devastating.

Being a church leader or marrying one doesn't give us the right to talk about someone else's business. Ever. Period. The end. We know how hard it can be, especially when the information we've been given feels nearly too heavy to carry. And sometimes we must speak up, such as when someone is trapped in an abusive situation or relationship. But that's not what we're talking about here. When we are frustrated over someone making poor decisions despite our pleas for them to change or simply sad because of a problematic situation, that's not a good excuse to reveal intimate details of a private conversation with a fellow staff member. Hashing out the gory details of what so-and-so got themselves into last summer is *never* a good idea. It will likely tear the body of believers down instead of building up. If you need to get something off your chest, find a therapist or a neutral friend with zero connection to your church.

From Gossip to Conflict Resolution

Some of you reading this are thinking, *You're preaching to the choir! I know this and abide by a no-gossip-out-of-my-mouth mentality.* We are thankful for you! But let's talk about this from a different perspective. What do we do when a church member comes to us with complaints about another church member? Sure, it's all good to lead them to offer grace or to defend the person being complained about, but perhaps we should be doing more to extinguish the gossip altogether. What if we used this opportunity to teach the Matthew 18 principle?

> If another believer sins against you, go privately and point out the offense. If the other person listens and confesses it, you have won that person back. But if you are unsuccessful, take one or two others with you and go back again, so that everything you say may be confirmed by two or three witnesses. If the person still refuses to listen, take your case to the church. (vv. 15–17)

God has laid out the exact steps of how to handle disagreements and conflict, but we tend to complicate what should be simple or ignore His Word altogether.

We know firsthand how devastating it is when a pastor skips that first step. Years ago, one of us found herself, with her husband, sitting across the desk from their former pastor. They were told that someone had complained about something she had said, but in truth she'd never said it. When she pleaded for the pastor to bring in the person who had complained about her so that they could work it out face-to-face, the pastor refused. He'd listened to the gossip and decided to manage the situation on his terms. But he did not follow what Scripture teaches us to do. If people feel free to state a complaint about a fellow church member to the pastor, they should be ready to approach the person they are complaining about. We, as church leaders, should insist on bringing everything to light. When we don't, we inadvertently feed the gossip, allowing our church members to believe something that may not even be true about their brother or sister in Christ.

Stop listening to gossip, church leaders. Just stop. Be bold enough to speak up for the person who isn't there to speak for themselves, and be willing to walk away from a hurtful conversation. And above all, teach Matthew 18 until the day you die. That sounds dramatic, we know. But the church is getting this wrong on so many levels, and sadly, church leadership carries much of the blame.

So, what does this look like? How do we make the shift and learn to disengage from gossip? First, don't talk about it if it's not your story to share. Period. Second, when church members complain to you about someone else, ask them if they've gone to that person first. If they haven't, graciously point them to Matthew 18. If they can't help but share someone else's business with you, graciously remove yourself from the conversation or change the subject.

You'd think this would all be Christianity 101 information, but even some more seasoned Christians and leaders in the church forget the fundamentals. So here we are, getting back to the basics. Perhaps we need this reminder:

> A servant of the Lord must not quarrel but must be kind to everyone, be able to teach, and be patient with difficult people. Gently instruct those who oppose the truth. Perhaps God will change those people's hearts, and they will learn the truth. (2 Tim. 2:24–25)

To be kind and patient, we must extinguish gossip before it spreads.

Keep Your Sexy Texts to Yourself

If we were to write down all the pointers we wish someone would have told us before we became pastors' wives, there is one piece of advice that would make the top of that list: always, and we mean *always*, double-check who is on the receiving end of every text you send. Trust us. Dear old saints like Elder Margaret or Deacon Joe will not find that sexy-time text meant for your hubby quite as humorous as you do—or maybe they will, but honestly, that would be gross and awkward.

Jessica learned (and perhaps is still awkwardly learning) this the hard way. Once, she accidentally sent a text meant as a laugh between friends—one that would surely make Grandma Betsy clutch her pearls—to a *large* group of church board members, prayer warrior saints, and none other than the bishop's wife herself. This story gets extra juicy because she owned it—and never retracted the text or told anyone she'd sent it accidentally. *Priceless.*

Sure, this story makes for great conversation and laughs around the table with friends, but for some people, such a mistake could be their last at their church. Church people can be ruthless. While some of us should be more careful about what we text and *who* we text, we also, at times, need an extra measure of grace applied to our mistake-filled shenanigans. Something we sadly don't always receive, even though many people expect to receive the grace they refuse to administer back to us.

———————

For all the sweet church people we genuinely love, please hear us when we say yet again that *we are not perfect and will make mistakes with our words, even in our texts.* None of us are immune to letting others down. But ultimately, this is just a solidly good reason to look heavenward rather than down at us little ole pastoral humans. Things will only be perfect once Jesus returns. This is not a novel concept, yet somehow we still get super disappointed when humans act like—you guessed it—*humans.* Mark it down, sis (or in the words of Stephanie's preteen boys, bruh): until Jesus returns, everyone we allow into our lives will disappoint us. But should we let what others do or say make us think less of who Jesus is? We sure hope not.

Pastors and their families can be pushed onto unreachable pedestals—like a wannabe social media influencer who presents a flawless highlight reel that leaves out the messy parts of life as their marriage and family crumble around them. Perhaps it's partially our fault for portraying a lifestyle that's the furthest thing from our reality. But people see and embrace *all* the positives, yet the moment we mess up and say something we shouldn't, we get judged in the same unhealthy manner no one else wants to be judged by. The pedestal comes crumbling down.

We've also been guilty of expecting people in leadership over us to never speak out of turn or commit any noticeable sins. We treat them like they are supposed to keep their mistakes swept under the rug . . . no need to stir up the dust by shaking it around to find what's hidden beneath. Instead, we could all gain from giving each other the benefit of the doubt. Empathy and compassion go a long way. What would others say about you if circumstances changed and your life was on display in fishbowl fashion? Perspective is everything.

As we hope and pray that our church families offer us grace and pause before they condemn us, some of us also need to be careful about how holier-than-thou our words come across to the people we counsel. We've seen, time after time, leaders attempting to overstep healthy boundaries church members have set for themselves by inserting their unsolicited and legalistic advice into how their congregants should run their homes, businesses, or personal lives. For those of you who have experienced this kind of toxic pastor or pastor's spouse, we want to take a moment to tell you we are *so* sorry you've had to tolerate such behavior. It's not okay *at all*.

Church leaders, we can do better, and we should! Yes, speak the truth. Step on toes when B-I-B-L-I-C-A-L-L-Y necessary. Do we need to repeat that for the people in the back? Only step on toes when it's absolutely, *biblically* essential and done with a true heart of love for your people. We cannot reiterate this enough.

As pastors' wives, we pray that God would use our mouths to point people back to Him. Perfection is not required, but a tongue filled with love, grace, hope, and pearl-clutching jokes sent via text only to the correct recipients is. And keep those foot-in-the-mouth moments to a minimum—if you can help it.

4

The Pastor's Wife
Wants to Skip Church
Sometimes Too

A day without a nap is like a cupcake without frosting.

—Terri Guillemets

Churches across the globe had to improvise when the world shut down because of the pandemic in 2020. It was a learning curve that caused both many setbacks and significant strides for the church's future. The pandemic was scary and stressful, but simultaneously it forced us to slow down in new ways. Potlucks, small group outings, and weekly church gatherings came to a screeching halt. These sudden changes must have been *so fun* for older, more traditional churches that still played cassette tapes on their thirty-year-old sound systems. Super duper fun. But the three of us found ourselves dusting off our favorite loungewear and cuddling up on the couch with our kiddos while we virtually watched our hubbies share the Word. The ministry world changed, and Sundays became quieter for many pastors' wives.

We have a confession to make, and it's a doozy. Although we missed our church family and did not want to be isolated at home forever, we *liked* not attending church in person every week. There, we said it. The truth is out, and we feel good about it! It might not sound like a polished PW thing to say, but we're sure you've caught on to the fact that we aren't those kinds of pastors' wives by now.

We get tired like everyone else, and the constant *move, move, move* mentality pre-pandemic was exhausting. We were happy to avoid whining kids who questioned why we had to go up to the church *again* and pleased to skip the formal pleasantries that accompany churchgoing and all the self-inflicted pressure. The couch became a close Sunday friend.

Why did we, deep down, enjoy this time of rest so much? Because we were burned out, plain and simple. Across the board, pastors, spouses, and ministry leaders are burning themselves out with all the activities, emergency calls, and emotional support they provide to their congregants 24/7. Extroverted or introverted, it's a lot for anyone to handle without breaks.

Of the three of us, Jessica has the highest intensity and propensity for doing *all* the things. She is often on the go and loves to lead and help where needed. But even with all the energy she naturally radiates, the opportunity to attend virtual church services from her couch relieved her. Being made to stay home was like being told she *had* to take a vacation. Or, more precisely, a *staycation*. Somebody grab this girl a pool float shaped like a flamingo and a fruity ice-cold refresher while she worships Jesus! Can we get an amen?

Looking back on those days of stay-at-home orders, it feels to Jessica like an angel fluttered down from heaven specifically to permit her to embrace Sabbath rest on Sundays. And perhaps many of us collectively breathed a sigh of relief when the world made us rest—you know, when we weren't fielding heartbreaking phone calls and sobbing church members who needed comfort during an unprecedented pandemic. (All right, one of us was also one of those sobbing church members, but overall, we still embraced Sunday morning virtual services in the comfort of our homes.)

When Every Day Is a "Yes Day"

Let's rewind a decade to when life was anything *but* sipping hypothetical daiquiris poolside. Jessica remembers well the pressure to say yes to everything. Do you need a counselor to ease you away from the edge of an anxiety attack at midnight? No problem, Jessica's your gal. Are you searching for a lady to lead the women's ministry Bible study? Jessica's on it. In the mood for an entertaining and relaxing girls' night for your small group? Tell Jessica the day and time, and she'll throw a themed soiree that would rival a Kardashian shindig (minus all the alcohol and cleavage).

This unrelenting pressure came from more than one source. Some of it was self-inflicted. Jessica believed being a good leader meant she needed to be busy. And isn't this the way most of us think? Busy equals productive, which equals the ideal servant of Christ, which equals Mrs. Perky Perfect Pastor's Wife. If this productivity math were true, then Jessica was slaying the pastor-wife-life.

On top of pressuring herself, Jessica often felt that her head pastor at that time would guilt-trip her whenever she, the youth pastor's wife, was not in attendance at a church function, even if she wasn't involved with that ministry. The head pastor's wife seemed to be allowed to miss events, but Jessica felt specifically targeted in this unhealthy church atmosphere. Because of his judgment, she felt she couldn't say no. (Side note: beware of pastors who manipulate or expect staff members to do what they won't do themselves. The best leaders are servants first. Let's keep our hearts in check as we minister in our respective churches.)

As if the pressure hadn't built up enough between Jessica's self-defeating thinking and the manipulation she felt from the pastor, some church members unwittingly heaped more on the already growing mound of pressure. When she did manage to skip a church event, people—who were likely concerned more than anything else—would question why she didn't attend. In Jessica's mind, these questions came across as disappointment rather than concern. Had these sweet people said, "We missed you," she might have felt differently.

Jessica isn't the only one who spent years saying yes to everything. Stephanie passed out yeses like pumpkin-shaped Reese's PB cups on Halloween (Let's face it, is there anything better?) because she dreaded disappointing her church and wanted to avoid the tragic possibility of *not* being recognized as the absolute best youth pastor's wife. Ever. And when she did start learning about healthy boundaries and used the word *no* on occasion, she felt guilty for doing so.

Image meant more to Stephanie than it should, and she craved admiration and approval more than anything. To put it bluntly, she was selfish. She made ministry about herself rather than keeping her priorities as they should be. Instead of putting God first and family next, followed by church ministry, her order went a little more like this: church ministry, church people, other people, other opinionated people, and finally, more people. God and family were afterthoughts during this tumultuous time.

No is not a dirty word, just as *yes* is not a sign of spiritual maturity. We can only utilize our yeses and nos well if our priorities are aligned correctly. Sadly, many of us have confused putting church responsibilities first with putting God first. They aren't the same thing, but we have blurred the lines so much that we no longer see clearly. The church is *not* synonymous with God. Yes, we are collectively His bride. And when we serve the church as Christ humbly came to serve us, we fulfill His call on our lives. But good things can go sour lickety-split when what we perceive as our "calling" precedes our relationship with God and the family He has given us.

The only time no isn't an option is when God definitively speaks to us. Otherwise, we can say no to things that would displace our most important priorities, even if they are good things. Church outreach activities can be a fantastic way to cover our community with love, which is very good. But just because it's a good thing does not mean we should participate every time. Deciphering good from *best* is a skill every church leader should master. There is wisdom in knowing the difference, and God's Word reminds us again and again of the importance of using wisdom.

> For the LORD grants wisdom!
>> From his mouth come knowledge and understanding.
> He grants a treasure of common sense to the honest.
>> He is a shield to those who walk with integrity.
> He guards the paths of the just
>> and protects those who are faithful to him.
> Then you will understand what is right, just, and fair,
>> and you will find the right way to go.
> For wisdom will enter your heart,
>> and knowledge will fill you with joy.
> Wise choices will watch over you.
>> Understanding will keep you safe. (Prov. 2:6–11)

What If Our Yes Is Their No

We hear a common complaint from pastors and their spouses: church people expect the pastoral family to do all the work.

But what if we have perpetuated this problem? What if all our yeses have kept those who need to step up from saying yes? Some people honestly don't think they can or should serve in some areas of the church. While some believe attending church services is all they need to do (after all, don't they pay pastors to do those other things?), others struggle with not feeling good enough or spiritual enough to lead or serve.

Some church members need a nudge to step into a new role. When that quiet couple reveals their hidden baby-whispering skills, perhaps it's time to point them to the sweet cherubs in the church nursery. If the man with the captivating smile has the uncanny gift of making strangers feel like family, why not invite him to join the welcome team? No matter the personality, everyone, deep down, desires to be seen. And when we go out of our way to notice others, it gives them the confidence to step up and serve the church in a whole new way.

We all have gifts to utilize and should be using them to bless each other:

> In his grace, God has given us different gifts for doing certain things well. So if God has given you the ability to prophesy, speak out with as much faith as God has given you. If your gift is serving others, serve them well. If you are a teacher, teach well. If your gift is to encourage others, be encouraging. If it is giving, give generously. If God has given you leadership ability, take the responsibility seriously. And if you have a gift for showing kindness to others, do it gladly. (Rom. 12:6–8)

Tales of Sickness Bliss

We feel guilty for mentioning this, but sometimes we relish the days when we are too sick to attend church. Years ago, Stephanie caught the flu and a domino effect of household illness followed, leading to Stephanie and her children missing three church days in a row. Was she sad about it? Not even a little bit. Cuddling her kids while a warm hug of covers enveloped her sounded like a dream. She felt no reluctance in being forced to lounge around with her sick kids for a week and a half. She could take off her metaphorical PW mask and breathe for once. She had no one to impress but her three littles, who were enamored by processed chicken chunks shaped like dinosaurs and all of Stephanie's ridiculous mom jokes. She could do no wrong in this scenario.

Yet this all made her feel very conflicted. She also felt disconnected from her church and carried a little cloud of depression everywhere. Regret and shame cut deep when Stephanie realized she enjoyed hiding away at home more than spending time with the church family she and Isaac served. How spiritual could she be if she wanted to hide from her and her husband's calling? But she's not the only one of us who has found relief when sickness hit her household.

When one of Jenna's children shows signs of being too sick to attend church, her gut reaction is to be annoyed at the inconvenience. She enjoys her Sunday church responsibilities and has no interest in skipping them—until she stays home and a massive invisible weight lifts straight off her chest. She wonders why they even attempt to ward off germs with handwashing techniques and cartoon-shaped vitamins when, all the while, they should be greeting viral infections and bacterial infestations with a hearty handshake. All right, she's not that crazy—and none of us want anyone getting sick—but she sure does savor quiet Sundays at home.

The Tropical Getaway Nightmare

It might be time for a getaway if you can relate to Stephanie and Jenna's tales of sickness bliss. Like any other working people, we need vacation time. Everyone requires intentional breaks. But when you make pennies, which is often the case when serving a church, taking a vacation is tricky. For the first decade of Stephanie's marriage, she and her family took zero breaks. Instead, they spent their vacation visiting family or friends within driving distance, with cell phones still wide open for receiving ministry-related calls. They were always "on," never allowing themselves space away from the demands of ministry life. They sucked their vacation time dry instead of turning off communication with the outside world and being present solely with their family unit.

Jenna remembers a specific instance when she and Ian were desperate for time away together. They hastily booked a trip to Cabo for their tenth anniversary, using a credit card to pay for the vacation. At the same time, they awaited their tax refund— not once considering the finances would never come. They were dumbfounded when they discovered they owed the government money instead of the other way around, a nasty shock to their systems. Regrettably, they boarded a plane using borrowed cash to attend a nonrefundable vacation they couldn't afford. Instead of fully unwinding and soaking in each moment of their trip, they wrung their hands as they contemplated how they would pay for this time away and what people would think about them squandering money on an elaborate vacation.

Nobody thinks twice when people with nine-to-five jobs board planes for tropical getaways, but when the pastor does it, we can start wondering if the church is paying them too much.

Here lies another reason why church leaders are burned out. We avoid time off because we fear the backlash of gossip. In a world where pastors can be criticized for wearing pricey sneakers, those of us who don't have dough rolling in from megachurches cower at the thought of receiving judgment from our church family or the outside world. So, rather than taking care of ourselves occasionally, we resort to doing more, going more, and reaching for more so no one assumes the worst of us. (Spoiler alert: they do anyway.)

We wish we'd realized long ago that time off is essential and doesn't have to cost a heap of money. The point is *rest*. If God included the Sabbath in the Ten Commandments and rested Himself after finalizing creation, then it's probably something worth noting (Gen. 2:3). Rest isn't a luxury; it's a command.

> Keep the Sabbath day holy.
>   Don't pursue your own interests on that day,
> but enjoy the Sabbath
>   and speak of it with delight as the LORD's holy day.
> Honor the Sabbath in everything you do on that day,
>   and don't follow your own desires or talk idly.
> Then the LORD will be your delight.
>   I will give you great honor
> and satisfy you with the inheritance I promised to your
>   ancestor Jacob.
>   I, the LORD, have spoken! (Isa. 58:13–14)

If we embraced this command, we might find joy in church ministry again.

How to Make Rest a Priority

As ministry leaders, we know our schedules should include rest. Forming a plan to rest may seem counterintuitive, but it might be the only way to make it happen. Get your calendar out with your spouse and block off days for time away. Make the plan and execute it. Set your phones on "do not disturb" and focus on each other and your family. We can hear the excuses now, and we are the queens of these excuses ourselves: "But what if someone dies or another emergency happens while we're gone, and no one can reach us?"

If there is an emergency, someone will reach you. If they could do it pre-2000s, before cell phones were the norm, they can find a way to get a hold of you now. You could even ask another staff member at your church to be the emergency contact if something unexpected and tragic happens while you are resting. Then your mind can be at ease. If there is a true emergency, this designated caller will inform you, so all other calls can go to voicemail. When rest becomes a priority, we find a way to make it work—one way or another.

In an ironic turn of events, one of us typed this chapter while snuggling with a sick child. The timing would seem inconsequential, except nothing we do as we spread God's hope is ever random or insignificant. So, the fact that she was stuck at home curled up under the covers, having missed one church service and other work-related tasks because of this unexpected illness, reminded her that she needed this lesson too. Despite knowing better, like a child who continues to reach her tiny fingers up toward the blistering stove, she ignored our advice and neglected to rest. And like the patient Father He is, God used His sense of humor to grant her the Sabbath she needed when she refused to take it herself. If you act like a toddler, He will treat you like one.

Sitting in an unplanned proverbial timeout is not quite as luxurious as a tropical getaway, that we can assure you. We wish we would stop doing the very things we encourage other pastors' wives and church leaders not to do. Like stubborn Paul, we get caught in a ridiculous cycle: "I don't really understand myself, for I want to do what is right, but I don't do it. Instead, I do what I hate" (Rom. 7:15).

We hate to hypocritically proclaim, "Do what we say, not what we do," so we will admit our missteps as Paul did. And then, as the adage goes, since we know better, we will do better. Will you join us?

5

~~~

The Pastor's Wife
Fights with Her Husband Too

I love being married. It's so great to find that one special person you want to annoy for the rest of your life.

—Rita Rudner

We represent a Disney-princess generation. Not the modern-day princesses like Elsa or Moana, who slay the bad guys singlehandedly with zero princely love interests on the horizon. No, we swooned over Prince Eric, Aladdin, and even the Beast sweeping their leading ladies off their feet and literally into their arms (or paws). We dreamed of flowing white gowns and a studly Prince Charming who would stand in awe as we floated down stately aisles into the start of our happily ever after. We were super cute.

But then we grew up and were aghast when we realized we'd married sinners who couldn't boast of royal paws—the nerve.

As we mature, fairy tales fade into the background of our minds, and we face reality. We are not princesses; therefore, our spouses are not princes. Are they good men? Yes! We are grateful, because we know this isn't the case for everyone. But as good as they are, they are indeed human.

Getting Honest about Our Imperfect Marriages

Even though we pastors' wives are keenly aware of our husbands' flaws, their negative traits aren't quite as apparent to the average churchgoer. Stephanie's friend from church casually commented one day that Stephanie's husband (the youth pastor) and the lead pastor of their church must be exceptional husbands. She was not being facetious. She assumed that since these guys knew the Bible well and taught other husbands how to treat their wives, they must be better at it than the average guy. We chuckled at her sweet naivety, because we know better.

One Sunday morning, while Jessica brewed coffee in the foyer of her church, a lady who attended came listlessly through the front doors with bloodshot eyes. Jessica immediately knew something was off, so she kindly intercepted this woman and asked if she could help. The lady began relaying the events that had her feeling out of sorts. She'd wasted her morning bickering with her husband and felt awful. In response, Jessica acknowledged how brutal such fights can be and pointed out how strategic the enemy is. He loves to attack believers who are on their way to worship or serve Jesus. Jessica admitted that she and Jonathan tend to have their most heated disagreements right before church or the night before. This sweet lady's jaw dropped, and she responded, "You guys fight too?" Jessica then began to open up about the explosive battles she and her husband had fought early in their marriage.

Twentysomethings Jessica and Jonathan were headstrong and stubborn. Each had different ideas of how conflict should be handled. Jonathan would separate and not communicate, while Jessica preferred a lively verbal skirmish until someone (we won't mention any names) finally admitted his fault. Jessica can recall pounding against closed doors with her fists while bawling, screeching, and reprimanding her husband when he'd retreated to another room during a marital showdown. If this sight had hit reality TV, ratings would have gone through the roof. Grab the popcorn, people. The Taylors are at it again.

When Jessica explained how she understood what the lady in the foyer was going through, this woman (normally quiet and introverted) began embracing vulnerability. She found the freedom to share her struggles because she now knew she wasn't alone. Shackles loosen when we share the truth of our stories.

Jessica has owned up to these rocky days of animated disputes with more than just this one lady in the church foyer. She and Jonathan have recounted their early days of feuds with many couples they counsel. Premarital counseling is riveting with the Taylors, that's for sure. The more they share, the more comfortable other couples become in sharing what happens behind the closed doors in their own homes. Just as James proclaims, healing thrives in moments like these. "Confess your sins to each other and pray for each other so that you may be healed. The earnest prayer of a righteous person has great power and produces wonderful results" (James 5:16).

Take Your Own Advice

Why can we be experts on giving advice, but when it comes to taking and applying that advice ourselves, we revert to being total amateurs? Marriage counseling is when we shine the brightest as expert(ish)-amateurs. Stephanie and Jessica have had plenty of moments where they've nodded in peaceful agreement with their husbands during counseling sessions while gritting their teeth and internally listing all the things their husbands *don't do* that they tell other husbands *to do*. But before they blurt out, "You big phony!" they remember that a counseling session for another couple is probably not the best time for an outburst. And before they can go the opposite direction and implode, almost always their hubbies surprise them by openly admitting their shortcomings.

Jessica will practically bore a hole through her husband with her eyes when Jonathan gives advice he fails to take. And in those moments, Jonathan quickly confesses that his wife is cutting him with her eyes because he struggles with this. Jessica appreciates her husband acknowledging his shortcomings in these sessions but wishes he would be as quick to admit his wrongdoing outside of counseling. She isn't the only one who has ever felt like this. But as we all know, plenty of fingers point back at you when you point at someone else.

Jessica will be midsentence, imparting her version of marital counsel, when the Holy Spirit whispers to her heart, *You know, you keep giving this advice . . . but when are you going to take it yourself?*

When we counsel, we need to be quick to draw a circle around our own two feet. Our guidance to others is sometimes precisely what we need in our personal lives. Dropping our pride to retain the advice is necessary. "Pride leads to conflict; those who take advice are wise" (Prov. 13:10). "Pride goes before destruction, and haughtiness before a fall" (16:18). As the Holy Spirit directs our mouths and guides our hearts with wisdom, He is teaching us too. He will break down walls and crumble barriers if we are humble and open to change. The Holy Spirit can heal us right in the middle of counseling someone else.

We wonder when it became so challenging to be honest about our imperfections. When did the church begin twisting Scripture so much that church leaders no longer felt free to confess their sins aloud to their church members? For example, when 1 Timothy 3:2 instructs overseers to be above reproach, it doesn't mean we should never admit our shortcomings. To be above reproach is to be Christlike with a level of maturity in our spiritual walk. How can we be either of these things without confessing our sins as the Scripture commands? Shame has enveloped what should be covered in grace. We fear that people may think differently of us if we talk about our husband-wife throwdown of the night before. Not to be insensitive or anything, but in the words of Jessica Taylor, "Who freaking cares?" People will always find the negative, but that should never keep us from doing what is right.

Posers on Pedestals

In the early years of Stephanie's marriage, she never shared any problems she and her husband had because she didn't want to be a stumbling block to anyone. Plus, she may or may not have thrived off people believing she had her junk together, thanks to her image-consciousness. But this facade came at a price. She felt alone in her faults and propped herself up on that unreachable pedestal of faux perfection we all should avoid.

God is bigger than our sins. If we believe His name will suffer if people see our flaws, we have taken an invincible God and attempted to shove Him into a box He is far too big for. God can handle Himself without our help. Sure, we should care about living lives that are pleasing to Him, but we will make mistakes along the way. We will royally screw up. We will be selfish in our marriages and act like total toddlers—repeatedly. But hiding our sins isn't doing God a favor. We aren't protecting Him from harm by hiding our actions. We're just trapping ourselves and adding to the illusion that pastors and their spouses hold the magic secret to unwavering marital bliss. No wonder we find ourselves exhausted from the Broadway-level dramatics we try to put on every day. We're exhausted even typing out this scenario. What in the actual Beaver Cleaver world are we doing to ourselves? Pretending is for posers. Perhaps we should let that sink in before permanently exhausting our marital reservoirs. It's not worth it. Period.

Recognizing the Enemy before It's Too Late

If you have served in church ministry for more than five minutes, you know when the most explosive fights tend to rear their ugly heads: right before preaching, serving, or counseling. It. Never. Fails. God's about to move, huh? Well, the devil, his helpers, and our flesh will undoubtedly be close behind. Let's not be surprised by it. We should expect it. We have targets permanently engraved on our backs. We are the best target practice for the enemy—and perhaps we should be clear about who the enemy is *not*.

Your spouse. Our spouses. They are *not* the enemy. They are targets as much as we are. Instead of getting distracted and engaging in friendly fire, we must direct our attention to the real enemy. We are much better off fighting together than fighting against each other. God intends for couples to be in this as one unit. "'At last!' the man exclaimed. 'This one is bone from my bone, and flesh from my flesh!'" (Gen. 2:23). Your "flesh from my flesh" is not the enemy. When your anger steams uncontrollably, take a beat to remember to aim your weapon toward your actual enemy.

For we are not fighting against flesh-and-blood enemies, but against evil rulers and authorities of the unseen world, against mighty powers in this dark world, and against evil spirits in the heavenly places. (Eph. 6:12)

We are meant to minister together, which sometimes means going to war together and for each other.

Ministering to people can be inconvenient and annoying when dealing with garbage in our own lives. (We were all thinking it, so we said it for you. You're welcome.) When an argument is cut short because we are needed at the church, it's nearly impossible to plaster on a smile and do the work that needs to be done. We like resolutions. A tidy ending to every uncomfortable conversation would be lovely. Still, we are messy people who don't store elaborate bows in our back pockets to whip out when one is needed for wrapping up an intense quarrel. Sometimes we must temporarily slide on our big girl pants and find a way to set our problems aside to serve someone else.

We get it. Putting yourself and your problems on the back burner is painful. But when it must be done, here is how you can move forward well. First, pray for your spouse and for your heart and mind. Then ask for patience, peace, and wisdom as you step into teaching, counseling, or whatever area of ministry you have next. Ask God to provide the peace that passes all understanding that He talks about in His Word. And above all, step aside and allow the Holy Spirit to move when you must move on. He can reveal the sin and a solution to you *and* your spouse. We need to get out of our own way. Stepping away from the situation can bring clarity and begin the healing process before you and your spouse even come back together to resume your "discussion."

The enemy would love to use these moments of tension, but you are not his for the taking. God is bigger than our disagreements and can turn these hurtful moments into something incredibly good. So, the next time you are interrupted mid-fight, don't fret. A little time apart can do more good than you think. "A hot-tempered person starts fights; a cool-tempered person stops them" (Prov. 15:18). Cool your jets and try again later.

The Abusive Pastor

Just recently, Stephanie read something in her child's devotional book that got her wheels turning. In *Indescribable: 100 Devotions for Kids about God and Science*, Louie Giglio begins one of his short devotions by describing an unusual flower.[1] Flowers are usually known for sweet aromas, but one flower will have your nostrils begging for release from its putrid death grip. According to Giglio, this flower, *titan arum*, has a memorable nickname: "corpse flower." Although *titan arum* is attractive on the outside, the stench permeating from its bloom will make you wish for an afternoon hangout in a middle school boys' locker room over breathing in its deathly aroma . . . well, perhaps that would be taking things too far. But the dramatic effect is on point, we think.

This flower reminds us all too well of some smooth-talking corpses posing as pastors. Their acting is phenomenal, but their walk with God is lacking if not altogether nonexistent. They are too busy making a name for themselves to acknowledge the slow, rotting death of their marriages. The church has become a magnet for narcissists. These leaders are careful not to leave any physical marks of their abuse, which can leave their victims to feel they have no choice but to suffer silently. Thankfully, more of these two-faced leaders are being called out for the metaphorical odor they leave, but still, too many of them go on abusing, unscathed.

Let us be clear: abuse comes in more than one form. Mental, emotional, and spiritual abuse can be as damaging as physical abuse. Just because a pastor is well-spoken and appears thoughtful and attentive to his congregants doesn't mean his home life is thriving. Some pastors' wives are drowning because of mistreatment—leading to depression, divisiveness, and for some, divorce.

Is every divorced pastor or pastor with marital problems a narcissist or an abuser? No. Some pastors are decent people who have neglected to find help for their struggling marriages. Either pride or a refusal to rest has slowly corroded the marital foundation. And others refuse to acknowledge the possibility of their spouse walking away one day. They get far too comfortable with the *for worse* section of their vows. Church ministry is draining. Without healthy boundaries, marriages die or half-live on their version of life support.

During the hard times is when those familiar verses in 1 Corinthians should be put to use: "Love is patient and kind. Love is not jealous or boastful or proud or rude. It does not demand its own way. It is not irritable, and it keeps no record of being wronged" (13:4–5). To be clear, no one can simply "love is patient and kind" their way out of an abusive situation. These verses help relatively healthy couples—those who have been struggling to love each other well and simply need counseling and better boundaries within their relationship to experience a thriving marriage.

When the Pastor's Wife Takes Second Place

When your job is serving church people, your home becomes a haven for just about everybody . . . except you. (Insert snarky side-eye smirk here.) Honestly though, our sofas have become therapy couches. Our tables have become youth-game-night hutches. Our porches transform into twinkle-light holiday venues. And while the three of us love that our homes comfort our church communities, sometimes we can get discouraged.

One day, a former youth group girl happily perched on one of Jenna's kitchen chairs as Jenna's husband, Ian, discussed the idea of a possible new ministry opportunity for her within his worship nonprofit. At one point in the conversation, Jenna took a backseat and curled up on the sofa while fiddling with her phone. As she casually listened to their discussion, hurtful, intrusive thoughts caught her off guard.

Ian patiently listened to this girl. *Really* listened. And he began asking more profound soul-care questions, like what goals she had and if she had been taking care of herself. Any decent youth pastor would ask these queries, but it got Jenna thinking. *Why doesn't my husband check in with me like that? Why doesn't he ask me deep questions and listen to my heart like he does for everyone else?*

A lump formed in her throat as she choked back the sadness and growing resentment she silently endured. She couldn't help but feel like her husband treated her differently than he treated everyone else—that the man she lived with had become someone she didn't recognize outside their home.

Instead of letting the resentment fester, Jenna approached Ian about her feelings. He's a good man, so he responded with understanding and love. He realized that what Jenna saw in him was accurate. He had been so busy pouring into everyone else that he could not pour into his wife. She would be there for better or worse, so he had been letting that relationship slide. After this conversation, Ian quickly made some much-needed changes around the home.

Jenna and Ian handled this situation correctly, but some pastors and spouses do not. Arguments erupt because the pastor is different at church than at home. Even good people who genuinely care can be two-faced. Pastors and ministers must be vigilant and remain self-aware enough to know when they are neglecting their homes for their church ministries. And their spouses need to do the same.

There is no magic cure-all for a pastor who abandons their number one priority. We are fully aware that we are preaching to the choir, er, preachers here. We might be cliché in offering some simple advice, but we will deliver it anyway. Are you ready to take notes? Don't have a pen? We'll wait . . . ready now?

Pray for your spouse.

We know, right? Your mind is blown.

And we aren't talking about the prayers you ramble at night before conking out pre-amen. We mean to go to war for your spouse in prayer. Pray over their pillow. Pray over where they walk. Pray over where they sit, stand, preach, and watch TV. Yes, there too. It doesn't have to be pretty or flowery language. It simply needs to pack a punch toward the enemy. Every day we fight a spiritual battle for and with our spouses, and prayer is our ultimate weapon.

Don't stop fighting for a healthy marriage. You have permission to choose each other over your church. You can be free from the pressure of presenting a perfect marriage. And you can speak up when your spouse forgets to do any of the above. You might not be married to Prince Charming, but isn't Kristoff better anyway?

6

The Pastor's Wife
Fakes Headaches Too

I saw my wife putting on her sexy underwear this morning. This can only mean one thing. It's laundry day.

—Anonymous

Now that the secret is out about our imperfect marriages, why not address one more warm-and-cozy (translation: *embarrassingly awkward*) topic? Hot-and-steamy sex lives are not the norm in pastoral marriages. We want to think that because we have devoted our lives to church ministry, God would sprinkle heavenly libido dust upon our sanctified loins, but that is not how it works. Pastors and their spouses face the same obstacles other couples do: hormonal imbalances, stress, fatigue, and, yes, even faking headaches because you don't feel like it, among other problems. Let's peek behind the facade of perfection to see what happens in our marriages.

But first, a story to set the scene.

Stephanie's father worked in landscaping for many years. He got the artistic genes in the family and could turn an average yard into a work of art that looked like it belonged among the manicured lawns of Disney World. But if you ever stopped by Stephanie's home growing up, you would never know it. Foliage, weeds, and grass nearly tall enough to conceal a small child consumed their yard. It was a jungle out there, folks! The problem with being great at something you do every single day is that by the time you make it home after all the work you've put in, you're exhausted and don't have the energy or desire to work on anything else remotely close to what you've done all day.

The same can be said of pastors. The emotional toll is heavy when you are on call 24/7 and spend your days counseling couples, building relationships with church members, and being one of the first people on the scene of a tragedy. Handling the emotions and needs of a spouse and children at the end of the day becomes too much. The pastor is exhausted. Their spouse is worn out. And sex becomes an afterthought. But this is not the only reason a couple may struggle with intimacy.

The Problem with Culottes

Let's take a trip back in time. The year was 1990-something, and the style choice for middle and high school girls everywhere (or at least in the South) was frizzball locks sort of straightened with a curling iron and white eyeliner smeared across upper eyelids, complete with plastic tattoo choker necklaces. Purity culture was in its prime, and a True Love Waits ring was found on every "good" Christian girl's finger to signify her promise to God, her family, and strangers far and wide that she was a virgin and would be so until the day she married the man her dad approved. CCM (Contemporary Christian

Music) was all the rage among evangelical teens, and DC Talk's hit "Jesus Freak" blared loudly and proudly from their boom boxes or burst their eardrums through the headphones of their Walkmans—or both.

Young Stephanie loved these glory days of evangelicalism, or so she thought. She tried to ignore the unnerving feelings bubbling below her smiley surface. She remembers one fiery camp meeting at her small, ultra-conservative church, which wasn't the kind of church fond of CCM or "Jesus freaks." Her church was filled with people who preferred hymns and women who wore culottes and kept to the meek and quiet way of life. If you don't know what culottes are, imagine two expanded parachutes, one attached to each leg. The word *flattering* does not come to mind.

As Stephanie was listening attentively to the guest preacher during the camp meeting's youth service, she was taken aback when this man walked straight to her pew, pointed his finger directly in her face, and hollered on and on something about the evils of "girls and their makeup." Teen girls who wore "worldly" cosmetics and followed the fashion trends of the day were targets in this religious society. According to this preacher, teen boys and even grown men could be sexually tempted by fourteen-year-old girls who dressed too "provocatively"—aka sans culottes. (Side note: if the thought of men being pedophiles disgusts you, we applaud you. We'll even take a break to hold your hair while you puke.)

Sadly, we grew up in a time when females and their bodies were described as the enemies of purity. Our guard could never be let down, because we could cause males to stumble with our God-given skin and beauty. Instead of resting in our fearfully and wonderfully made bodies, we hid them behind unflattering parachute pants and prayed we wouldn't "lose our purity" or "cause a man to sin," as if we have anything to do with making ourselves pure. Last time we checked, only Jesus's blood can make us pure from every sin.

While Stephanie endured finger-pointing and the dreaded culottes phase, Jessica had a different yet equally horrifying experience. A male teacher at her Christian school thought he would take a teachable moment to compare her and her classmates to an Oreo. Everyone loves a good Oreo, right? Or at least happy people—have you ever met a happy person who hated Oreos? But we are getting off-track. Jessica's teacher held a scrumptious Oreo in the air for the class to see, twisted the decadent treat in half, and then nibbled off some of the creamy icing in the middle. Now, brace yourself if you are squeamish. He then passed the cookie to a student nearby and had them lick off some more of the icing. The students passed the Oreo around the classroom for every person to lick or nibble on until it was too disgusting to handle. Apparently, germs were cool in these pre-COVID times.

This teacher went on to explain that each of the students was like a delicious Oreo. And when they had sex outside of marriage, they became more like the cookie that had been snacked and slobbered on. The more people they gave themselves to, the more disgusting they became. Who would want the used Oreo?

Jenna grew up with similar experiences as Stephanie and Jessica. She heard a never-ending message that sex was wrong and we should never do it outside marriage. Without even realizing it, she took the idea to heart that her body was also sinful. Every time the youth group would swim together, the girls were forced to wear oversized, baggy T-shirts over their swimsuits while the boys were allowed to wander around shirtless, because these Christians believed that boys were visual creatures and girls weren't. According to this "logic," boys are sexual but girls aren't, and they shouldn't have the same burning desires as boys. Whether it was the church's intention or not, these thoughts permeated Jenna's mind and made her feel ashamed of her body.

How Purity Culture Harms Healthy Marriages

Purity culture did a number on all three of us. It affected each of us differently, but the hurt bled into all of our marriages. Stephanie bore tremendous pressure when she became a wife. Logically, she knew sex with her husband was expected, healthy, and God's plan, but her body screamed something different. She could not shake this strange underlying feeling that she might be doing something wrong. It took years for her to understand the guilt she sensed and why she experienced it.

Jessica had learned another destructive message: a good wife had to have a sufficient amount of sex with her husband to keep his eyes from straying to another woman or being tempted by pornography. Her marriage would suffer if sex didn't happen often. But as we all know, ministry life is hectic. Throw in a couple of kids and it gets even crazier. When Jessica and Jonathan could not be intimate multiple times a week like purity culture taught, she feared her marriage would be damaged. Even after considering every area of their relationship and realizing their marriage was relatively healthy, she couldn't shake the internal messages she'd absorbed from purity culture.

Jenna dealt with her insecurities when she got married too. Once she and Ian tied the knot, she could barely contain the excitement. But when having sex didn't meet her expectations, disappointment hit hard. Her sex drive dropped, and she became self-conscious about her husband seeing her naked body. Those days of purity talks had taught her brain and body that sex was wrong, and she struggled to break free from that message playing on a loop in her brain.

The Balance of Churchy Sex Ed

As ministry leaders, we have collectively done the church a disservice on the topic of sex. We distort Scripture, turn the topic of modesty into a weapon against women, and fail to provide our young couples with healthy conversations on marriage and sex. We have either shouted from the rooftops that s-e-x is *bad*, or we've taken a more modern approach that sex is fantastic . . . too bad you can't do it yet. (But in case you do, here are some condoms and birth control.) Where is the middle ground?

Purity culture thrived on shaming teenagers for their mistakes and spreading the message that losing your virginity is the worst sin you could commit. Sure, you can receive forgiveness from God, but you can forget about offering the greatest gift to your spouse. You ruined that chance and might as well tattoo a big fat scarlet *A* across your forehead.

What if instead of attempting to scare teens into making the right choice, we tell them the truth? Sex is a gift from God for husbands and wives. God created this beautiful gift to accompany intimacy and love within marriage. He never intended for unmarried people to have sex, and the natural consequences God established for partaking in this good gift at the wrong time will play out when we don't follow His way. The Word makes it clear that these are God's intentions for marriage: "Give honor to marriage, and remain faithful to one another in marriage. God will surely judge people who are immoral and those who commit adultery" (Heb. 13:4). Conviction will come. Pregnancy before you are ready or diseases are always possible, not to mention much greater heartache if the relationship ends.

Teens also need to know that 1 John applies to this sin too:

> But if we confess our sins to him, he is faithful and just to forgive us our sins and to cleanse us from all wickedness. (1:9)

My dear children, I am writing this to you so that you will not sin. But if anyone does sin, we have an advocate who pleads our case before the Father. He is Jesus Christ, the one who is truly righteous. (2:1)

Mistakes happen, but God forgives every single one.

Along with telling them the truth about sin's consequences, we should spend more time educating our children about sex before they hear a distorted version from their friends or the world. Keeping an open dialogue with our children could be the key to more teenagers choosing to wait for marriage and having healthy mindsets about sex when/if they tie the knot. Education is vital. "Teach [my commands] to your children," the Lord instructs us. "Talk about them when you are at home and when you are on the road, when you are going to bed and when you are getting up" (Deut. 11:19). The responsibility to teach our children lies with us. We cannot neglect it.

Jessica's mother openly and honestly shared with Jessica the mistakes she made before marriage and expressed how great sex was within marriage. Jessica never felt embarrassed about asking her mom about sex because her mother embraced the questions and answered without reservation. Because she heard healthy messages from her mom regularly and knew the consequences of giving her body to someone other than her husband, she waited eagerly and did not have sex before marriage. Unfortunately, the overwhelming purity lessons Jessica learned from her church and Christian school gave her so much anxiety about meeting the "frequency of sex" mark with her husband that it took her a long time to remember the balanced messages her mother taught her.

As church leaders, it's our privilege to walk alongside parents in our church as they disciple their children at home, but many of the books and curricula we have suggested to our church people in the past have wounded otherwise healthy marriages. We must use discernment when offering advice and should be careful about perpetuating messages that are harmful to ourselves and our children. We highly suggest Sheila Wray Gregoire's book *The Great Sex Rescue* for anyone curious about the destructive aftermath of purity culture and which books on sex and marriage are doing more harm than good.[1] Sheila also wrote *The Good Girl's Guide to Great Sex*, and, with her husband, Dr. Keith Gregoire, *The Good Guy's Guide to Great Sex*; both are great alternatives for newly married couples.[2] We also suggest The Whole Story Video Course for teens and preteens, which will guide parents in healthy conversations about sex.[3] These resources are excellent; we hope more church leaders will recommend them to their congregations.

Pastors and Porn

Being in the late stages of the third trimester of pregnancy is rarely the most confident period of a woman's life. Some feel sexy until the end and rock bikinis with their sun-kissed bellies for all to see. We salute you, brave ones. But for the rest of us who feel more like beached whales than sun-bathing goddesses, the third trimester can dampen our sex drive.

When Jenna's belly expanded as new life grew in her womb, she never considered sporting a bikini. Her third trimester would be void of a bare beach belly, and that sucker would be pasty white from the lack of UV rays; you could guarantee it. She didn't want her husband to see her body, let alone strangers. Because of her insecurity and those pesky pregnancy hormones, sex had zero appeal. This awkward time in her life brought back to her mind an issue Ian had dealt with before marriage.

Back when Jenna and Ian were only dating, he admitted to struggling with pornography use in the past. He had reached out for help, though, and had set accountability measures in place. Once they got married, Jenna never thought about that past issue and assumed it would never be a problem for him again. But one day far along in her pregnancy, while she fought her lack of sex drive, something prompted her to ask Ian if he had looked at porn during their marriage. The prompting must have been Holy Spirit–led, because he admitted he had viewed it during her pregnancy.

Jenna was crushed. Sadness, anger, and shame hit in waves, lapping up all her remaining confidence and security. She blamed herself for being a super-unattractive wife who barely ever wanted to be sexually intimate with her husband.

Here is another lie that purity culture taught so many of us: it's our fault if our men look at porn. We are the problem, and we should be the solution to their porn usage. Nope, nope, nope.

The truth is, Ian struggled with this sin before he even knew his wife. It had nothing to do with her. After that conversation, Ian set up measures of accountability again, and the two of them walked through the healing process together. Today, Ian has found freedom and is on guard against the temptation.

Jenna's husband allowed us to share this personal story to help anyone else who struggles with this sexual sin. In 2016, the Barna Group surveyed pornography use and found that 21 percent of youth pastors and 14 percent of pastors admitted they currently struggled with using porn. About 12 percent of youth pastors and 5 percent of pastors said they were addicted to porn.[4]

Being a pastor or a spiritual leader does not mean you are immune to porn or other vices. As you can see from the statistics, porn use is more common among the clergy than many realize. And these numbers are only based on the men who were *honest* about their porn use. We cannot turn a blind eye to church leaders (women included) being bound by sexual immorality. Church leaders need accountability in all areas. If they shrug it off, red flags should be flying. "Fear of the Lord is the foundation of true knowledge, but fools despise wisdom and discipline" (Prov. 1:7). Only fools refuse wisdom. And too many pastoral marriages suffer behind closed doors because of sexual sin void of accountability. "Plans go wrong for lack of advice; many advisers bring success" (15:22).

Intimacy Is More than Sex

Since we began hosting our *Pastors' Wives Tell All* podcast, we have built many new relationships with female church leaders worldwide. Through getting to know these women through social media DMs, emails, and our Facebook community group, we are finding more and more pastors' wives whose marriages are on the rocks because of a lack of intimacy (not just the act of sex). We've already expressed the negative impact of purity culture and pornography use, but those two are not the only reasons for a lack of sexual intimacy.

Church leaders seem to be resilient, but that's only because we are pros at being chameleons. What you need, we've got. But tirelessly pouring out emotional, spiritual, and physical reserves can transform spouses from soulmates and best friends into roommates who tolerate each other only because they made a vow. If this is you, don't panic. If your spouse is spiritually and emotionally healthy and loves you and God fiercely, there are simple ways to grow your intimacy.

Jessica and Jonathan endure extended periods of high stress and little sleep. Most days, they collapse onto the bed in the evening with zero energy for any marital extracurriculars. They have learned that sometimes they can't help but bring home baggage from the day and be affected by its weight, despite knowing they should "leave it at the door." Instead of feeling guilty over these dry spells, they've learned to focus on spending quality time together and have realized their marriage is healthy despite the draining moments.

Intimacy is so much more than having sex. Jessica now uses a different metric in her marriage when a taxing season hits. She asks herself if they are still communicating—real, deep, honest communication with each other. Are they laughing? Playing card games has become a favorite stress reliever that gets them roaring with laughter together. They dance in their kitchen, hold hands while going on walks, take an interest in each other's hobbies, and touch each other during the day (foot massages included). If the communication, laughter, and non-sensual touches keep happening during spells of fatigue, then sexual intimacy will come again after they get some much-needed rest.

Your marriage will not go off the rails if there is balance. And when the bedroom becomes spicy again, learn to be comfortable in your skin. Keep laughing and stop taking yourself so seriously. You can get stuck in a rut simply because you've become complacent. When you quit having fun, it shows in the bedroom.

Again, sexual intimacy is more than the act itself. The needs we read about in our Bibles go much deeper.

> The husband should fulfill his wife's sexual needs, and the wife should fulfill her husband's needs. The wife gives authority over her body to her husband, and the husband gives authority over his body to his wife.
>
> Do not deprive each other of sexual relations, unless you both agree to refrain from sexual intimacy for a limited time so you can give yourselves more completely to prayer. Afterward, you should come together again so that Satan won't be able to tempt you because of your lack of self-control. (1 Cor. 7:3–5)

In the King James Version, verse 3 is translated "Let the husband render unto the wife due benevolence: and likewise also the wife unto the husband." The word translated as "benevolence" originates from the Greek eunoia, which according to *The New Strong's Exhaustive Concordance of the Bible* means "kindness, good will."[5] Kindness and goodwill go deeper than a primitive, sensual need. In *The Bible Exposition Commentary*, Warren Wiersbe makes an interesting statement about these verses: "The wife's body belongs to the husband, and the husband's body to the wife; and each must be considerate of the other. Sexual love is a beautiful tool to build with, not a weapon to fight with."[6] The sexual experience within marriage should be utilized with kindness and with the purpose of building intimacy in the relationship. None of that happens if we selfishly think only of our own physical passions. True intimacy is selfless.

Years ago, one of Stephanie's friends told her how badly she struggled to let loose during sex when she and her husband were newlyweds because her past mistakes weighed on her heavily. Instead of her husband getting frustrated with her timidity, he prayed over her in bed. He loved her and wanted her to find healing and freedom in their marriage. Things began to change for the better as they prayed for their sexual intimacy and intentionally focused on it.

It might make us feel about as awkward as a middle schooler with bacne at a swim party to pray about sex, but why should it? Repeat after us. Sex is holy. Sex. Is. Holy. S-e-x is *holy*. Or at least it is when you experience it with your husband. Since most of our readers are pastors' wives, we're pretty sure you're doing it with your husband. (If not, well, then we could suggest a whole different book for you, and perhaps a therapist.)

To wrap it all up, we don't always feel sexy. We will face obstacles in our marriage. We might even hit roadblocks because of sin. But we can be the ones to make a change. We *can* have healthy sexual intimacy with our spouses. We can break free from the burdens of the past. And we can teach the next generation how to walk in sexual freedom with their spouses.

PS: They say practice makes perfect. So why don't we all take a quick break from reading? Get comfortable in our skin. And begin practicing what we preached this entire chapter. A shirt, shoes, or even pants are *not* required. (Wink, wink.)

7

~~~

The Pastor's Wife
Questions God Too

The important thing is not to stop questioning. Curiosity has its own reason for existing.

—Albert Einstein

Applying for your first job is nerve-racking. Whether you're a teenager seeking to save the cows as a Chick-fil-A team member or a college student inquiring about the internship of your dreams at a prestigious law firm, putting yourself out there in any capacity is daunting. But when Stephanie and Isaac anticipated the results of the most crucial church vote of their new life together, they were oddly at peace. Sure, there were a few butterflies-in-the-stomach moments, but they were convinced that *this* city and *this* church were where they would start their lives and ministry together. They were following Jesus, so there was no plan B. Oh, how blissfully ignorant these two pastoral babies were. (Hey Google, play "What Dreams Are Made Of" by Hilary Duff.)

Stephanie and Isaac never accounted for the humanness of the church members. As Isaac answered the phone call that would reveal their fate, Stephanie squealed like a little girl and leaned in for an animated high five or a bear hug, or any other over-the-top exuberant reaction from her husband. But instead she watched his smile deflate and be replaced with a mouth hanging open in shock. They needed a 75 percent yes vote from this church to get the youth pastor position, but they received 74 percent. In that moment, 1 percent never felt so astronomically massive.

The man on the other end of the phone tearfully recounted the sobering events of that Sunday evening. A few families who'd attended the church for years had reservations about spending the money to hire a youth pastor. But instead of mentioning their concerns earlier in the process, they'd waited until the night of the vote to address them, and the results were devastating.

That night they attacked, and things spiraled out of control. The members of this church family turned against one another, spouting accusations and pointing fingers until the church imploded. Within the week the pastor resigned, and the church split all because a few families waited until the night of a church vote to express their true feelings. Stephanie was stunned by it all and left with a host of questions. *Why would God lead us to this place when He knew this would happen?* She couldn't understand how they could be so sure of the Holy Spirit's leading but end up somewhere completely different from what they thought was the will of God.

This would begin many more twists, turns, and heartaches that stirred up more doubts in Stephanie's mind. Becoming a pastor or a pastor's wife doesn't mean you'll never experience uncertainty. Spiritual warfare is intense when you follow God, no matter your calling. Questions and fears arise at the most inopportune times . . . like 3:00 a.m. when you should be drooling into your pillow, not reevaluating your entire life's purpose and wondering *why* God thought creating humans was a good idea, because the church would be *so* much better without them.

But God always has a plan. He's working behind the scenes even when all His kids have lost their minds. He isn't surprised by any of it. In fact, He promises in His Word that He is working out the details for us.

> "For I know the plans I have for you," says the Lord. "They are plans for good and not for disaster, to give you a future and a hope." (Jer. 29:11)

> "My thoughts are nothing like your thoughts," says the Lord.
> "And my ways are far beyond anything you could imagine.
> For just as the heavens are higher than the earth,
> so my ways are higher than your ways
> and my thoughts higher than your thoughts." (Isa. 55:8–9)

No matter what our lives look like in the moment, God hasn't lost control.

When Obedience Stings

Some girls grow up toting around baby dolls and making lists of their favorite baby names. We're talking the expansive lists with both boys' and girls' names, first *and* middle—along with a substantial backup list . . . you know, in case they end up with twentysomething kids and counting (minus the reality TV show and the scandal). You never know. A girl's got to be prepared for every scenario. But other girls are too busy squashing bullies on the playground or crushing boys on the basketball court to stop and think about future babies. Who has time for kids when you have plans to be the first female president of the United States? Jessica was the latter.

Jessica and Jonathan were all in when they dove headfirst into youth ministry, so their house became a home away from home to a multitude of teens. When people would ask when they were planning to start a family, they'd say they already had kids—a *ton* of them, who were eating them out of house and home. Why on earth would they want babies? (This might be the perfect time for us to mention that asking couples when they plan to start a family is never a good idea. Some couples desperately desire children but have not yet been able to conceive them, and others simply desire a different path. Jessica and Jonathan were the latter.)

Time passed, and the desire to give birth to children never came. A different longing stirred within their hearts and grew as their love for missions expanded. God planted a simple thought that would take root and grow their family (minus the morning sickness and epidurals): they would cross oceans to find their babies. Literally. Their first baby girl was born in Russia, and the second in China.

But the road to international adoption is not easy and can be astronomically expensive. We're talking tens of thousands of dollars per child. Jessica and Jonathan were living on a one-person income—a youth pastor's income, no less. But they knew God had called them to adopt their children, so they pressed forward, not knowing how they could ever afford them.

We've all heard stories of God waking a believer in the wee hours of the morning with a mission to bestow a large sum of cash on a person or specific organization. Many times, the person hearing the voice of God doesn't even know why they need to give, but they walk out their obedience in faith and gift the money regardless.

Well, we're not sure where all these people went during Jessica and Jonathan's adoption journey, but it seems crickets were the only ones chirping in those early-morning hours. Nobody heard the blessed monetary call from the Lord.

The financial burden was significant, and Jessica had more questions than answers. *Why are people not motivated to help us with this adoption process? Is God not speaking to them? Are they not listening?*

Why can't we catch a break with grants? We're always denied.

Why won't our lead pastor share about our adoption journey with the church family, but he will share from the pulpit about his own child's adoption?

The questions pummeled her mind until she ached. She wondered why God would allow seemingly selfish people who refuse to give to charitable causes (but toss their money at frivolous things) to get paid thousands upon thousands of dollars (even millions) while people who love Jesus and are serving Him with their lives remain locked on the pecuniary struggle bus. It wasn't fair, and she whined to God with all her pessimistic musings. And even when some sweet people gave to their adoption fund, and others helped later in the process, she couldn't see clearly through her righteous indignation. She focused more on the ones who wouldn't give than those who gave, forgetting that no matter how small the gift, it all helped.

Slowly, God began to shift her mindset. He never promised that His path for us would be smooth (I mean, have you ever heard of Paul or Job?), and she learned to embrace this truth. God softened Jessica's heart and is still at work on her today as they pay off the debt of those two precious baby-turned-tween girls. Rather than allowing her eyes to wander to what everyone else is *not* doing, she is more introspective now. She recognizes the joy in obedience whether anyone else comes along for the journey or not. Our acts of obedience aren't for people to notice. They are all for the glory of God. She understands Habakkuk more now than ever:

> Even though the fig trees have no blossoms,
>> and there are no grapes on the vines;
> even though the olive crop fails,
>> and the fields lie empty and barren;
> even though the flocks die in the fields,
>> and the cattle barns are empty,
> yet I will rejoice in the LORD!
>> I will be joyful in the God of my salvation!
> The Sovereign LORD is my strength!
>> He makes me as surefooted as a deer,
>> able to tread upon the heights. (3:17–19)

When Grownups Act Like Toddlers

We all have secrets. Now, before anybody gets all riled up, let's breathe. We can hear you retorting, "I am an open book. Always. No secrets here." You can be an open book yet still hold some secret thoughts. Or at least the three of us sinners do. As the years trudge on, we become more aware of the secrets, some silly and some depraved, that always seem to lurk in religious circles.

As kids who grew up in church, we were happily oblivious to the quarrelsome or lousy decision-making of the grownups who led us. We thought that when we turned eighteen, the childish bickering, unrestrained anger, and even the girl drama would all dissipate, and we would officially cross the threshold into peaceful, sensible adulthood.

Plot twist. We grew up, became pastors' wives, and the truth came to light. It turns out that adults create their own cesspools of drama. Who knew? And church leaders often get a front-row seat to all the theatrics.

If we are in ministry long enough, the weight of everyone else's drama piles atop our own, and the conflicting ruminations can spin wildly out of control. We begin to question if all of this is worth it. People can be so unreasonable, ill-mannered, hot-tempered, and selfish. We don't want to give and give and give to people who expect us to move mountains for them when they refuse to budge a molehill.

When church hurt surprises us, we want to know why God sent us there. Why did He allow unhealthy leaders and pastors to serve alongside us? Why didn't He rain fire down on the adulterous pastor on our staff? Why are we sent to a church that is slap full of jerks while other pastors get all the praise? But Habakkuk shows us we aren't the only ones with these questions: "Must I forever see these evil deeds? Why must I watch all this misery? Wherever I look, I see destruction and violence. I am surrounded by people who love to argue and fight" (1:3). (#Relatable.)

All of us imagine what life would be like if we worked regular, everyday, nine-to-five jobs, where we left our projects at the door when we clocked out. Reality is distorted, so we complain and wring our hands in exasperation over serving people who seem undeserving. But then the Holy Spirit knocks our prideful hearts down a few notches and reminds us of the truth.

God declares to our hearts, *Because you are worth it, they are worth it too.* We are as broken, if not more so, than the people who complain to and about us. Our sin is just as ugly as theirs. We deserve forgiveness to the same degree they do. And we *can* "taste and see that the LORD is good" (Ps. 34:8).

He works *all* things for good. Not *some*. All. "And we know that God causes everything to work together for the good of those who love God and are called according to his purpose for them" (Rom. 8:28). We may never see this good purpose with our own human eyes, but we trust in the One who is working behind the scenes on our behalf. He continues to guide His children, just as He always has:

> I will lead blind Israel down a new path,
>   guiding them along an unfamiliar way.
> I will brighten the darkness before them
>   and smooth out the road ahead of them.
> Yes, I will indeed do these things;
>   I will not forsake them. (Isa. 42:16)

Lessons Learned at the Youth Retreat from Hell

We all know someone who always has the wildest, most out-landish, over-the-top, terribly awful story to share. Have you had a bad day? So what. They've had one epically worse. You've got stories? They've got bestselling novels. Your cat got run over by a car? Well, their two dogs, five chickens, three guinea pigs, and the canary they nursed back to health following a fateful fall from its nest and losing its wing were all consumed in a devastating house fire lit by the deranged pyromaniac who lived next door.

Even though such hair-raising tales give us pause, occasionally we hear harrowing stories that turn out to be true. We want you to know that the following tale is not an attention-seeking narrative. It is the true story of Jenna and Ian's youth retreat from *hell*.

The year leading up to this wretched weekend had been no magical rainbow affair. The retreat was simply the moldy icing atop a stale, maggot-infested cake. Jenna and Ian had been try-ing for that year to get pregnant, but month after month, Jenna stared down upon only one pink line that reminded her once again that her body would not cooperate . . . or maybe God didn't hear her prayers. Anyone who has faced infertility for any amount of time will understand their state of mind.

With infertility weighing heavily, they prepared to depart on the weekend retreat. At this time, Ian was the youth pastor *and* a worship leader for the youth group—both unpaid positions—while he worked full-time as a teacher. They were feeling underappreciated and taken advantage of, but they pushed forward.

The drama launched as they took to the road with their sizable group of teenagers. They stuffed as much luggage as possible into Jenna and Ian's vehicle and squeezed the teens onto a school bus. The road trip went flawlessly for a whopping thirty minutes . . . or an hour . . . or maybe two hours. (We don't remember the time frame, but you get the point. Things went wrong in a hurry.)

Jenna rode along with the teen girls on the bus as Ian served as the pack mule, his car weighed down by all the baggage he carried (literally, but also figuratively). Then one of his tires burst under the weight of the luggage. No one on the bus noticed, apparently, because it kept trucking along as Ian slowed to a bumpy stop on the side of the road. To keep things extra interesting, the breakdown was far from the nearest city and Ian had zero cell service. Nada.

Thankfully, his car stopped in the yard of a sweet older couple who did their best to assist Ian as he changed out the blown tire for the spare, but he had to singlehandedly remove every suitcase from the car and place it on the side of the road to be able to lift the vehicle enough to change out the tire. Did we mention this was no small group of kids?

Meanwhile, as Ian sat on the side of the road with no cell service, the bus arrived at the hotel, where they ran into roadblock number two. The perplexed hotel clerk searched for a reservation booked under their name. She found none. Ian had made the reservation online using the church's credit card, which he couldn't access on this trip. When he finally arrived at the hotel, Ian and Jenna desperately tried to reach anyone they could think of at the church who could help them, but not a single person answered their calls. They finally bit the bullet and put the expense on their personal credit card.

By nightfall they were drained, but, as with all teen trips, they barely rested all night. After a very trying and tiring day one, their hopes of a fresh new start were dashed when they woke to a bus that would not start. Day two began with a bang. Thankfully, a friend of theirs happened to be attending the same retreat with their own group of teens and volunteered to shuttle their group to and from the camp hosting the retreat (twenty minutes there and twenty minutes back). His van would not hold their bus's capacity, so they had to take several trips.

When the final set of teens set off for their day, Ian headed to the nearest auto parts store to purchase a bus battery. If you've never bought a bus battery before, be grateful. The total cost sucker punched Ian in the gut as he once again pulled out his personal credit card (while the church leaders continued to ignore their phone calls).

The day dragged on, unaffected by this string of "bad luck" until nighttime hit. Then a storm began brewing (and we aren't speaking figuratively). The clouds circled overhead, and then the bottom fell out. The camp staff didn't realize some kids were still waiting to be picked up. They shut off the lights and left them standing outside in the dark, soaking wet, waiting for the van to make its rounds while the rain pelted down.

The cherry on top of this eventful day was when the students decided to play pranks on one another later that night. But these were no typical, all-in-good-fun pranks. These were acts of vandalism. Kids were sneaking out of their rooms, overturning beds, and damaging property. Jenna and Ian were fuming, and Ian spent the night correcting these youth group delinquents.

On the last day, when they'd filled their gas tanks and started the trek home, Ian and Jenna noticed something strange. Black fumes began to spew from the bus's exhaust pipe. Then full-fledged flames replaced the smoke at a stop light. Come to find out, a fuel mix-up caused the fire show. Someone had filled the bus with diesel instead of regular fuel.

Finally, after dropping the teens off with their parents at the church, they could not jump into their vehicle fast enough. But this would not be the end of their adventures. On their way home, their car died multiple times—an oddly appropriate metaphor for their weekend. It was so ridiculous that it was comical. (Or at least it is now, years later.)

Just before collapsing onto their bed, Ian activated the home alarm system and locked their bedroom door. Mind you, it was 1:00 p.m., slap dab in the middle of the day. Jenna stared at him, bewildered, as he explained that it wouldn't surprise him if someone broke into their house or drove a car straight through their window. He refused to take any chances. Ian called in sick to work on Monday. Technically, he may not have been physically ill, but he sure was sick of life, sick of students, sick of things going wrong, and exhausted.

———

Jenna and Ian could not for the life of them understand what God was doing. Why would He be silent as the church took advantage of them and they struggled financially? Why would He allow the enemy to wreak havoc over their students' retreat? And why could they not start a family? They were drowning in their tears of sorrow.

Back up to the previous evening: Jenna had been angry with God for a while over their infertility, but something changed that last night at the retreat. As teenagers gave the sins and worries they had been holding on to over to the Lord, symbolically writing them down on slips of paper and throwing them into the fire, Jenna knew God was asking her to do the same. She gave her anger, hurt, and desire for a baby over to Him as she watched her slip of paper burn to ash.

She still had questions. She didn't understand why this season of ministry was so grueling, but she felt more at peace with her circumstances. And as all seasons do, this one would come and go.

The day following their return from the retreat, as Jenna scurried around her bathroom getting ready, she decided to take a pregnancy test. She took one every month, but this time felt different. She didn't fret over the result. She didn't expect a positive test at all. Thinking it would be the same as always, she placed the test on the counter and kept moving. When she finally took a second to glance at it, she let out a shriek. She was staring at two pink lines. Two!

After all the waiting, the agonizing, the anger, and the tears, God answered with a gift. Jenna surrendered her desire to have her own kids to the Lord, and in His goodness and mercy, He allowed them to have children. We are keenly aware that this is God's plan only for some. We don't always receive the things we think we need. He sometimes has a different plan, and His plans are always good even if they feel painful in the moment.

God reminded Jenna that He is trustworthy. He never left them. And in His timing, He performed a precious miracle.

> The Lord hears his people when they call to him for help.
> He rescues them from all their troubles.

The LORD is close to the brokenhearted;
    he rescues those whose spirits are crushed.

The righteous person faces many troubles,
    but the LORD comes to the rescue each time.
        (Ps. 34:17–19)

We all face adversity in ministry. There's no reason to feel guilty about asking God questions as we wrestle with trauma and frustration. We didn't inherit superpowers when we became a pastor or pastor's wife (unless whining is a superpower. We've got that down pat). Ask the questions. Fight the flesh. And don't you dare give up!

(Hey Google, play "The Champion" by Carrie Underwood.)

8

~~~~~

The Pastor's Wife
Yells Too (Parenting PKs Ain't No Joke)

Raising kids is part joy and part guerrilla warfare.

—Ed Asner

The enemy stinks. *You heard us, Satan. You stink.* Sometimes you've just got to tell it to him straight. The enemy loves to get into our heads, and he's done a number on us recently. As we were prepping for this chapter and compiling our thoughts on parenting our precious PKs (pastor's kids), pandemonium broke loose. Our little cherubs morphed into monsters, while their mothers (bless us) transformed into tyrants . . . or at least our PKs thought so. We could pretend this wasn't a perfectly timed, strategic attack from the enemy, but we refuse to be that ignorant.

The enemy wants nothing more than to keep us from writing these words of life over you and your kids. He wants to destroy the ministry your family has committed to, starting with your family unit. Why have so many PKs run as far as they can from the church and their relationship with God? Because they are targets. And we are sometimes the vessel the enemy uses to push them away.

Quick side note: in order to protect the privacy of our children, we will not be calling any of them by name or sharing any specific details about them as we discuss parenting.

You Don't Actually Suck at Parenting

Parenting is one of the most beautiful gifts God created. The responsibility of discipling kids to grow up to be godly humans is rewarding, yet also one of the most arduous tasks we will ever be assigned. We could attempt to dress it up with glitter, rainbows, and promises of unusually obedient kids, but we speak the truth around these here parts (and occasionally use Southern speak). Parenting can be the absolute worst. No one prepares you for the sucky volumes in your parenting story. But good times or bad, not a single person or method could efficiently prepare you to raise your child because they're *yours*, no one else's. They aren't that other child raised by the Mother Teresa of all moms. Every child is unique, and every parent will hold a bundle of joy uniquely crafted for them—a child different from every other human. You being your child's parent is no mistake or happenstance.

Whether our children came to us through our womb or adoption, God chose us for this. However, this doesn't mean we'll always get this parenting gig right. Just ask Jessica.

"One day, God's gonna give you a child *just like you*." These words came rushing back as Jessica battled her headstrong child. She'd been a stubborn, argumentative teen, but she never imagined she would one day build her family through adoption yet somehow still end up with a child who took after her. (God is a comedian. Don't let anyone tell you otherwise.)

That week, if anybody had asked Jessica if she was a good parent, she would have laughed in their face and replied with a hearty, "No, I suck as a parent. I'm doing a *horrible* job." Haven't we all experienced those weeks? We start believing that God might make mistakes, because this parent-child pairing is no match made in heaven.

As dreadful of a parent as she feels she is during times like this one, Jessica realizes her feelings aren't the truth. She's not a bad parent. Imperfect, yes, but not *bad*. Motherhood has ups and downs. That week she happened to be on a downward slope. At times she's been annoyed with her kids and even admits to not *liking* how they're acting despite *loving* them with all her heart. But the love she has for her children always ends up overshadowing their misbehavior, and she remembers that she is the God-chosen woman and her husband is the God-chosen man for bringing up these children God's way. They are the people for the job. And you are too. God set it all in motion before you were even conceived:

> I knew you before I formed you in your mother's womb.
>> Before you were born I set you apart
>> and appointed you as my prophet to the nations. (Jer. 1:5)

> You watched me as I was being formed in utter seclusion,
>> as I was woven together in the dark of the womb.
> You saw me before I was born.
>> Every day of my life was recorded in your book.
> Every moment was laid out
>> before a single day had passed. (Ps. 139:15–16)

The Stigmas That Need to Die

There are two opposing stigmas that pastors' kids inevitably get stuck with. Either they are the worst kids in the church, partying it up on the weekends and giving even hypocrites a bad name, or they are the children who put grown people to shame with their expert knowledge of the Bible. Do you need to know Habakkuk 2 in the original Hebrew? The PK has your back.

How are our kids ever supposed to succeed with such pointed assumptions? Why can't they be afforded the space to make mistakes and learn from them, just like other kids? One reason we may treat our kids differently is surely because of the pressure we feel from others.

When Stephanie's children were young, she strove to be the best at *everything*, including parenting. She desperately desired for the people in her church to love her kids, so if they ever acted up, she would react in one of two ways: reprimand them much harder than they deserved and differently than she would discipline at home, or attempt to hide the behavior so that no one would notice. She didn't want her kids to be *those* pastor's kids. Jenna has responded similarly to her kids acting up at church. Usually, she attempted the duck-and-run scenario. *Get the hooligans out of sight before anyone notices.*

We're sure many other parents make these mistakes with their children, but it seems there is added pressure for pastors in this area. Church people have decided that when the pastor's kid acts up, it's a direct reflection of their parents. If the PK gets too rowdy, the pastor must be doing something wrong. Our kids are held to a higher standard than other churchgoing kids. And as they get older, they begin feeling that pressure deeply.

Our children had no say in our calling. The three of us either started serving in church ministry before we had children or when they were very young. They didn't ask for this life but were tossed straight into it. Instantly, expectations were placed on them and us and began poisoning our parenting. When we focus on cleaning up our kids' outsides so they are the ideal preacher's kids to everyone else, we lose them. A temporal, legalistic standard will replace a lasting passion for Jesus. And the first taste of freedom they get, they'll kiss all those rules and regulations goodbye, along with the church and our Savior.

If we could look you straight in the eyes and offer you one piece of tough love advice right now, we would say this: *You have nothing to prove. Absolutely nothing. You are not required to prove yourself to others. God approved of you when you accepted His Son's sacrifice and started a relationship with Him. Period.*

Our primary objective as parents is to introduce our children to Jesus and raise them to be God-followers. Nowhere in the imaginary PW handbook does it say that our kids must be perfect.

Let's go ahead and accept the fact that our kids will act like kids. Our teenagers will act like—you guessed it—*teenagers*. They will mess up in front of church people. They will face the consequences of bad behavior. They will grow and trip and fall flat on their faces a time or two million because they are learning life from scratch. None of this should affect our parenting. If we unfairly berate our kids, we will hinder them, as Colossians teaches: "Fathers, do not aggravate your children, or they will become discouraged" (3:21). And honestly, the church should offer all the PKs a little grace too. Our kids need it.

Living That *Little House on the Prairie* Life

Sometimes we wonder what life would be like if we lived a *Little House on the Prairie* type of existence. Back when families read together, had zero cell phone interruptions around the dinner table, and lived a slower-paced life. But then thoughts of slavery and death by smallpox come to mind, and our nostalgia dies a sudden death. But the point is, "busy" has become our churchy motto. And so much more so when it's our job to be there.

Our time can be rapidly consumed with everything from potlucks to women's ministry meetings to youth outings to a bazillion other church activities. Where does this leave our children? It's great to include them in ministry, because every ministry opportunity is another learning opportunity. But where do we draw the line? Pastors' kids easily fall through the cracks when their parents get so busy serving everyone else that they forget their first ministry. We cannot sacrifice our children on the churchy altar we've constructed. They burn out on church when they get placed on the back burner. Resentment can take hold of their vulnerable hearts when we run to everyone else who's hurting before we even see their hurt.

If a church member needs us, we drop everything to be with them. We grieve with them, listen to them, and offer counsel to help them process and move through their heartache. But when our children are hurting, are we as quick to do the same for them? How often have we dropped everything to be with them and allow them to process their emotions, even when it gets messy? We tend to tell them to dry it up and put on their big girl or boy pants. Their meltdowns are inconvenient and selfish . . . but not the church people's breakdowns. *Those* are important. Or at least this is the message our kids receive.

Stephanie finds it nearly impossible to stop moving. If it's on her to-do list, it's getting done, even if her kids get pushed to the end of the list. She realizes this about herself and is attempting to be better about putting her list aside for her kids.

One night, a college student from church called, needing to bounce around some thoughts with Stephanie. But when the time for this college student to arrive for their talk came near, one of Stephanie's kids fell apart. This kiddo needed Mama, so she immediately texted the student and asked if they could meet at a different time that week. And you know what? The world didn't collapse because she altered her plans. But her child's world became much brighter and more secure, knowing Mama would be there even when it wasn't convenient.

Our children are the most critical ministry God has given us. Let's not neglect it. Love them first. Choose them first. And like the Scripture says, teach them first:

> And you must commit yourselves wholeheartedly to these commands that I am giving you today. Repeat them again and again to your children. Talk about them when you are at home and when you are on the road, when you are going to bed and when you are getting up. (Deut. 6:6–7)

We can't "repeat them again and again" to our kids if we neglect spending time with them. They must take priority.

So What Does Daddy Do, Anyway?

We live in a world of extremes. A black-and-white kind of world that doesn't embrace the gray so much. This thinking bleeds over into parenting PKs. We've seen two different outcomes with pastors' kids. One, they are thrown headfirst into ministry life, knowing too much about Brother Johnny's drinking problem and the heated debates on whether changing the sanctuary's carpet would be sacrilegious. (*Gasp!*) Two, on the other end of the spectrum, they are kept clueless about what their dad does and have no idea why he goes to the church to "work." Who does that?

Jenna recently realized that she and Ian had never explained to their kids what Daddy does. They never told them the story of God calling him to ministry and his answer in obedience. They never conversed around the dinner table about how God was working through their family, whom they got to help, and how the kids got to be a special part of all of it. When it hit Jenna and Ian that some of the behavior issues they faced from their children might be due to a lack of communication, they shifted.

They sat their children down and explained how their family was in ministry together. They shared how, as their kids, they also had an essential role in the ministry. Sometimes that looked like sharing Daddy with the church or inviting others into their home. They also addressed spiritual warfare and how Satan did not want their family to be close and unified. He desired nothing more than to tear them apart and cause misery in their home. They allowed the enemy to win when they gave in to self-defeating thoughts and feelings.

Conversations like these are healthy and necessary for parents in ministry and for their children. The family unit is in trouble if the communication halts or never begins. We must find the balance between our kids knowing nothing about the ministry we're called to and knowing too much. There is wisdom in teaching our children about what we do and why we do it, without the added awareness of church drama. Proverbs insists gaining wisdom is wise, so shouldn't we desire this for our children? "Getting wisdom is the wisest thing you can do! And whatever else you do, develop good judgment" (Prov. 4:7). We can help our kids gain wisdom from the start.

How to Teach Our Kids about the Enemy

Who remembers the days when bullying meant giving swirlies in the germ-infested high school bathroom or slapping "kick me" signs onto the backs of unsuspecting targets? Nobody wanted to be the kid wandering about with a sign on their back. For us, those days are forever seared into our memories (and nightmares).

Today's bullying might look a lot different, but many of us are still clueless about the sign marking our backs. There's a bull's-eye flashing brightly on our families that the enemy targets. Every Christian is a target, of course, but when you take your faith further and serve your church, community, or other parts of the world, your bull's-eye might as well be one of those obnoxious neon signs blinding every passerby.

We weren't surprised when our kids were plagued with thoughts of worthlessness and hopelessness the week before we wrote this chapter. Something like that happens every time God is up to something big. When mission trips, church services, meaningful podcast conversations, weekend church retreats, or anything else spiritually positive is on the horizon, we know an attack is imminent. The enemy is sneaky, but we've got him figured out. He uses the same old tactics every time. Sadly, some fail to recognize his attacks.

Jessica refuses to leave her kids defenseless to the enemy. She began talking with her kids about the reality of spiritual warfare way earlier than most parents would, but she was determined to arm them for battle before they were caught by surprise. Sure, this ongoing conversation has been heavy, but her goal is not to raise "sweet little girls." She is training warrior princesses who will boldly stand up for what is right and change the world for Christ.

We could make the excuse that our children are too young to hear about how the enemy works, but we are not promised tomorrow. We have only today, this very moment, to teach our children how to fight. Jessica lives in the now, constantly reminding her girls that their part in the church is just as important as Mom's and Dad's. They have a purpose and a calling and are part of the body of Christ as soon as they accept Christ as their Savior. They don't have to wait to be active. And even though they are not the pastor, they are a pivotal part of the ministry.

We have a choice. Will we arm our children for the battle raging around them, or will we pretend that spiritual warfare is nothing more than a cute song and a thing of the past? As if the enemy stopped his attacks once the Bible was complete. *We're not Paul, so we must be good to go, right?* Friend, the battle is still active. Not knowing about spiritual warfare doesn't protect our kids' innocence. It only makes them vulnerable to an attack.

We can prepare our families for war. It starts with communication. Please talk with your kids about your experience with spiritual warfare (using discretion and speaking on their level, of course). Know the signs of the enemy and practice spotting his tactics. Memorize Scripture as a family that can be used as a weapon and a shield. Become familiar with the armor of God outlined in Ephesians and encourage your kids to put it on every single day. The enemy is real. He is ugly. He is coming to destroy every bit of who you are and who your kids can be. The faster you realize what he's trying to do, the faster you'll take him down.

And above all, teach your kids to replace the enemy's words of destruction with God's words of life. Memorize this Scripture:

And now, dear brothers and sisters, one final thing. Fix your thoughts on what is true, and honorable, and right, and pure, and lovely, and admirable. Think about things that are excellent and worthy of praise. (Phil. 4:8)

Then arm them for battle:

Be strong in the Lord and in his mighty power. Put on all of God's armor so that you will be able to stand firm against all strategies of the devil. For we are not fighting against flesh-and-blood enemies, but against evil rulers and authorities of the unseen world, against mighty powers in this dark world, and against evil spirits in the heavenly places. (Eph. 6:10–12)

Memory Lane is a fun place, but let's not lose our way and get trapped in its antithesis, Nightmare Alley. Swirlies and the like can stay exactly where they belong . . . in the deep, dark past—also known as *the '90s*. We are no longer targets. We are the sharpshooters. Being the butt of Satan's jokes is *not* part of the game plan. And the enemy doesn't stand a chance with our children!

We can't forget that our children are God's first. Our job is not to mold them into good little rule-abiding clones but to point them to a lasting relationship with Jesus. Ultimately, they must decide if they will follow Him or reject Him. Whatever decisions they make, we are to love them fiercely, just as God unconditionally loves us.

9

The Pastor's Wife
Goes to Therapy Too

To form meaningful connections with others, we must first connect with ourselves.

—Brené Brown

Adulthood is way overrated. Sure, there are perks, like eating a colossal amount of ice cream without permission or going out whenever you want to because you answer to no one (besides your scrawny ghost town of a wallet). Overall, being a grown-up is more glamorous in theory than it feels in practice. We've heard that growing old is like becoming a fine wine, getting better with age. But most days we feel more like a lukewarm cheap beer than a classy glass of Chardonnay. Profound, we know.

And part of becoming an adult, they say, is that all the childhood trauma you experienced comes back to haunt you in your thirties. We're unsure who *they* are or where they found said research, but they know things we don't. The anxiety, repressed memories, and emotions we have now are like air filling a balloon. We (the balloons) helplessly collect the blustery carbon dioxide while adjusting ourselves to handle the escalating pressure. Only the air keeps expanding our thinning, rubbery surface until it becomes too tight and fragile to hold it anymore. It bursts; we explode. And being a church leader can compound the explosion.

What Anxiety, Hives, and Cheese Curds Have in Common

Stephanie is complicated. On one hand, she gets incredibly awkward when people cry (*super* convenient when you counsel teen girls). On the other hand, she herself is acquainted with emotional breakdowns consisting of cheese curds, mint Oreo custard from Culver's, and a good Netflix binge while attempting to hold it all together . . . and failing. Years of conflicting emotions and copious losses have culminated in a body and mind riddled with anxiety and hives (literally). Her breaking point hit in 2010.

The year started hopefully for Stephanie and Isaac. They were expecting their first son in June and had begun nesting (as much as you could nest in the olden pre-Pinterest days). They thought they were ready, but *What to Expect When You're Expecting* didn't cover what to do when you grieve three losses in one year and experience postpartum depression concurrently.

First, Stephanie lost her grandpa (her Papa and childhood Super Mario Bros. teammate). This loss ended a chapter, since she had already said goodbye to her grandma (aka Grammy) a few years before. But the sadness didn't end there. As she grieved her grandparents, her lovable mutt, Roxie, faced a health crisis. Following a misdiagnosis and multiple seizures, the vet did everything they could to save Roxie's life. But her mysterious antifreeze poisoning had gone too far—an unsolved mystery (they still don't know how she was poisoned). The tears were a flood by this point.

A break in the sadness came with the arrival of her baby boy, a squishy-cheeked ball of cuddles *and* colic. Stephanie was happy, but a cloud of depression began to form—hardly noticeable at first. Something wasn't right, but she couldn't put her finger on it. Unfortunately, it wasn't long until she faced the most difficult loss of all.

She got the call on July 31, 2010. Stephanie and her sweet boy were snuggling in the nursery glider chair, the only position her fussy boy relished, when her cell phone rang. The words *stage 4 colon cancer* combined with her best friend's name made zero sense. How could this be real life? The following two and a half months were a whirlwind that abruptly stopped when her best friend met Jesus face-to-face. Stephanie dealt with the pain the only way she felt she could survive, by pretending it hadn't happened. She called her best friend's phone and listened to her voice on the voicemail daily, choking back tears, for months. But instead of facing her devastation, she wedged herself into her big girl pants the only way she knew how and continued trucking—for the next decade. But repressed feelings usually find a way to surface, even if they look different than you'd expect.

After Stephanie's debilitating anxiety was born in 2010, intrusive thoughts and compulsive behaviors began, followed by autoimmune issues a few years later. But everything changed during a podcast interview in 2022. As a guest on the show recounted her battle with obsessive-compulsive disorder (OCD), everything Stephanie had been experiencing for over a decade clicked into place. Maybe she couldn't bootstrap her way out of this. Maybe she did need help.

So, Stephanie dropped her pride and embraced professional advice. The thought of being on a daily medication for her brain had always unnerved her, but she took the Zoloft plunge when her doctor suggested it. As time went on, her mind slowly quieted. Her thoughts became clear, rational, and calm for the first time in years. When her friends and family noticed the shift in her, she wondered why it had taken her so long to take care of her mental health. Those years of panic and illogical thinking could have been avoided. But the negative churchy opinions she'd heard about medication and therapy had been ingrained in her mind.

Why Counseling Isn't a Last Resort

Once upon a time, *therapy* was a dirty word. You heard it spoken only in hushed tones, with a solemn head shake. But we have entered a new phase, one where therapy is what all the cool kids are doing—or at least most of them. But once again, it's different for church leaders. In some churches, therapy still has a negative stigma. You can't have a relationship with God *and* go to therapy or take medication for anxiety or depression. That would knock the pedestal of perfection over and set it entirely ablaze. This is why it took so long for Stephanie to step foot in a mental health facility, and also why Jessica believed the stigma for years.

When Jessica counseled married couples, she noticed that most people seeking counsel were at their breaking point. They were usually on the verge of divorce (or a murderous end worthy of its slot on Lifetime TV). These were some dire straits, people. Jessica thought this was normal for couples seeking counseling: they had to be a hot mess to qualify for therapy sessions, naturally. But what if counseling isn't meant to be the last-effort problem fixer? What if it's the path to avoid murdery messes entirely?

In her early thirties, Jessica had to discard everything she thought she knew about people who went to therapy or counseling. They weren't the exception or the oddballs who couldn't get their lives together. They were and *are* you and us. Therapy is for healthy people, not just those riding the struggle bus.

Leaders process about a million and one emotions, our own and everyone else's. As much as we want to pretend that the stories, traumatic experiences, and losses we walk others through won't affect us in the long run, they 100 percent do! And carrying that stress from other people's lives can become a crushing weight if it goes unaddressed. If we want to care for our temple—mind, heart, and soul—then isn't it good to seek wise counsel?

Counselors come in many forms. We need prayer warriors to stand in the gap for us. We need counselors to offer an empathetic ear and truth-filled words, ones who will get down in the dirt with us and drag our tails right back out of the guck. We need teachers, therapists, spiritual directors, and mentors to guide us as we lead others.

Knowing everyone's secrets and sins is a heavy burden to bear. We think we can handle it or that it is just the cross we are supposed to carry, but no human being can absorb all the drama, trauma, and heartache of others without imploding. Look to Proverbs and see what happens without wise counsel: "Without wise leadership, a nation falls; there is safety in having many advisers" (11:14). We need a safe space to let it all out. When that load is finally released, we are set free.

A book wouldn't be a book without controversial statements. Hey, that sentence alone is controversial. For the peacekeepers reading this, don't close these pages just yet. We aren't getting any crazier than we have thus far. But here goes: *only some people need a professional therapist.*

Does everyone need a counselor? Absolutely. But does your counselor need to have a degree? Well, it depends. If your anxiety or depression is out of control or your family and friends are telling you to seek help, get yourself to an actual professional. But if you are in a season of good mental health, finding one or two safe voices in your life can be profitable and provide you the necessary counsel.

Jessica doesn't meet with a professional therapist at this point in her life. She has in the past, but her counsel now comes from a different source. She runs to one or two trustworthy people in her circle when she needs to unload any strife, hurt, or weight from other people's baggage. These confidants are wise and follow Jesus closely. She can process with them and walk with them. She allows them into sacred places of her life to which others have zero access. But she doesn't let just anyone in.

How to Choose Wise Counselors

Many people can offer advice quickly, but some should never be given a proverbial podium. It is easy to attract spiritually shallow individuals who affirm us as we wallow in our sins and muck. But we need truth-tellers who will bruise our egos and snatch us out of that defeatist pit. We don't need yes-people in our lives. We need people who will hold us accountable, people who will walk through the fire with us and cheer for us on the other side.

Our minds should be guarded by a fence: not a literal fence, but a mental one. This fence should be tall, comprehensive, and impossible to penetrate without entering through the gate. You are your mind's gatekeeper. You must protect your mind with the tools God has given you and always be careful whom you allow to enter. Before impulsively swinging wide the gate to a potential disaster of a counselor, ask yourself a few questions:

1. Does this person walk with integrity? "For we are taking pains to do what is right, not only in the eyes of the Lord but also in the eyes of man" (2 Cor. 8:21 NIV).

2. Do they listen more than they speak? "There is more hope for a fool than for someone who speaks without thinking" (Prov. 29:20).

3. Is this person a gossip? "A gossip goes around telling secrets, but those who are trustworthy can keep a confidence" (11:13).

4. Do they speak the truth even when it's hard? Are they the kind of person who holds their people accountable? "Instead, we will speak the truth in love, growing in every way more and more like Christ, who is the head of his body, the church" (Eph. 4:15).

5. Do they embody empathy and compassion? "Finally, all of you, be like-minded, be sympathetic, love one another, be compassionate and humble" (1 Pet. 3:8 NIV).

6. Is this a person who desires to truly hear others? Are they tuned in to the person confiding in them or selfishly thinking of what they will say next? "[Do not be] looking to your own interests but each of you to the interests of others" (Phil. 2:4 NIV).

7. Is this a person of prayer? "I urge you, first of all, to pray for all people. Ask God to help them; intercede on their behalf, and give thanks for them" (1 Tim. 2:1).

8. Do they possess a gift of discernment, with the ability to read between the lines of what you share with them? "And it is my prayer that your love may abound more and more, with knowledge and all discernment, so that

you may approve what is excellent, and so be pure and blameless for the day of Christ" (Phil. 1:9–10 ESV).

Jessica confides in a woman who meets all these criteria. Shortly before we began this chapter, she contacted her about a tough week of parenting. This counselor listened and permitted Jessica to admit aloud that her week plain sucked. Yes, that exact word choice. At first, she was hesitant to claim the awfulness of the situation. She knew she could easily get lost in a tailspin. But her wise friend thoughtfully responded, "I get where you're coming from, but I also know you. I trust you know the difference between falling into old habits and admitting this is hard." Her friend reminded her who she was in Christ while pointing her back to the Holy Spirit for guidance. This is the kind of counselor we all need, whether a paid professional or not. We are in a spiritual war and cannot be victorious without counsel: "So don't go to war without wise guidance; victory depends on having many advisers" (Prov. 24:6).

What Our Children Teach Us about Ourselves

Our children are tiny mirrors. When we look at them, we see much of ourselves reflected. We don't like to admit it, however. We swiftly reprimand their bad attitudes and sarcasm when, just the day before, we expressed how *excited* we were to find their dirty underwear on the bathroom floor or how we *live* for the opportunity to clean up after them. It's *the best* part of our day. (And we wonder where they get it from!)

Jenna's life changed when she and Ian decided to seek help for their overly anxious child. The counselor they visited was attentive and insightful. He suggested they have their kiddo tested to find the root cause of the anxiety. This began their journey of parenting a child with ADHD, but it was also the tipping point of another startling discovery.

While Jenna scanned the internet for resources to help her understand her child better, she investigated why people with ADHD do the things they do. She asked friends with ADHD a plethora of questions and discovered something about herself as she sought to care for her child.

Many children diagnosed with ADHD have a parent or family member with ADHD too. Jenna immediately assumed Ian must be the culprit. His leaving-cups-all-over-the-house self was surely the root of the problem. It's funny how we can be staring straight at our own reflection yet insist we see someone else's.

As she devoured ADHD articles and resources, she realized that *she* related to the descriptions of ADHD tendencies in adult women. Could it be possible that she had ADHD too? (But to be fair, she was half right. Her hubby did end up being diagnosed with it too.)

For years leading up to this discovery, Jenna was anti-medication. Or at least against the type of pharmaceutical drugs explicitly created for the brain. She was down with the ibuprofen and the antacids (a girl has needs). But after birthing babies, her anxiety skyrocketed. Her mom noticed the struggle and casually mentioned that she might benefit from anxiety medication. Jenna dug her heels firmly into the hill she'd set her grave upon and pushed through those days of baby blues.

Years passed, and her anxiety, underlying frustration, and inability to be present when working on tasks all worsened. Jenna was in her midthirties before she realized medication could be beneficial. She made an appointment, got diagnosed, and began her healing journey on ADHD meds. The difference was evident almost immediately. She was less distracted and more present when family and friends shared their hearts with her. She felt more empathetic, occasionally tearing up in conversation (which was never a go-to response beforehand). Her anxiety became manageable, and she wondered why she had let stigma or other people's opinions deter her from medication. Doing what was best for herself and her family while following God's lead was the right move for her situation.

Is medication for everyone? No. Is it possible for our anxiety to have spiritual roots rather than physical—or a combination of both? Absolutely. But none of us can peer into someone else's mind. When we abrasively advise an anxiety-ridden friend, family member, or church member to get right with God or pray harder to feel better, we are amplifying the problem, not helping.

As with every topic we address, there is nuance to this conversation. It's not cut-and-dried. In the church, we shouldn't shy away from these serious conversations on mental health. People want to feel heard. And we should always listen with Holy Spirit discernment. Yes, sometimes our church friends need tough love, but those conversations should be handled with care and a ton of humility and prayer. In the end, what matters is seeing people the way Jesus sees them, opening our eyes to the person behind the problem. He can provide wisdom to decipher the difference between a healthy person needing a nudge and an unstable person genuinely drowning in their mental mess. We can change the church's tainted view of mental health. It all starts at the top, and ultimately, it begins with the reflection in the mirror.

10

~~~

The Pastor's Wife
Needs a Friend Too

You don't have to be crazy to be my friend. I'll train you.

—Anonymous

Finding friends as a pastor's wife (or any church leader) can sometimes feel like you're the new kid attempting to find a seat in the cafeteria on the first day of school. As you bob and weave between tables, praying to God nobody notices your awkward, new-kid-without-a-clue vibes, you end up losing your balance, sending the tray holding your school-chosen meal ("healthy" cheese pizza and a foreign, mushy, green substance the cafeteria staff assures you is a vegetable medley) sailing into the air. You hit the floor with a thud, and every eye in a twenty-foot radius gawks at your green-mush-covered self. You would be a cautionary tale as old as time, except there is no cautionary tale about making friends in the ministry—only platitudes and praise for this prestigious position you are blessed to serve in.

Where's the warning about the green-mush-all-over-your-face-type situations in ministry? Where are the tales of profound loneliness? Well, they exist, and it's time we talked about them.

The Lie Keeping Us in Middle School

We could write an entire book on relationships. But we will avoid the urge (for now) to turn this chapter into a novel about the drama we've encountered with complicated friendships. You're welcome. We want to home in on just a few areas where church leaders become paralyzed over finding and developing friendships.

A lie has been passed down from one pastor's wife to the next. It has been shared as holy truth when it's nowhere to be found in the Bible. This advice seems helpful and like it is in our best interest, but it isn't. Here it is: *you can't have friends in your church when you are in the ministry.*

If you have never received this advice, count yourself blessed. It's about as helpful as the air fluff setting on the dryer. (Sorry not sorry if that's your favorite setting. But please share your secrets, because we are baffled by the notion of fluffing sans heat.) Back to the point: at first glance, we understand that this statement seems like solid wisdom, but it falls short.

Sure, some people will use you when you hold any place of leadership. And it can feel scary to open yourself up to the possibility of a parasitic friendship, because these folks will do what they can to further their agendas. They draw you in with their kindness and overwhelming "generosity." They may even lavish you or the church with monetary gifts and extravagant favors. Some people are genuinely that generous. But others have ulterior motives, and the moment you hold a boundary with them or turn them down for a position they seek, they will turn on you like bad salmon on an empty stomach. It isn't pretty.

Before we send you screaming in the opposite direction of all church friendships, hear us out. Yes, friendship can be tricky. We need discernment to choose who can be trusted as a close companion. But it is possible to build your community among your church people.

We have all walked through times when friendship seemed impossible. One of us didn't want it, while another desperately desired it but could not make it work, no matter how hard she tried. But we've learned from our experiences and found sweet friendships both within and outside our churches.

No church leader should feel like the new kid in middle school. Been there, done that, trashed the T-shirt, and refuse to return. Goodbye, cafeteria mush, embarrassing falls, and acne. We are done with *all* of that, except maybe the acne (darn these nearly fortysomething hormones).

Your People Are Not in Your Comfort Zone

Jessica never really liked other women. And yes, she knows she is one. Despite living in a world of gender confusion, she's good in that department. And maybe we're exaggerating with the *never*, so let's back up. Jessica has always had a few close female friends, but she could relate to guys more quickly and loved how easily they could get over disagreements. They'd fight and then high-five afterward and continue their lives. The drama of middle and high school friendships with girls left a bad taste in her mouth as she entered adulthood and ministry. Some had been finicky, petty, judgmental, and gossipy, and she figured it would be the same for adults in the church.

Now, she's not entirely wrong. But this does not describe every woman. That stereotype needs to go! We could get off-track, but we will avoid taking the heated rabbit trail of how we've been brainwashed into believing *all* women fit into that cliché. Just understand that while some women may share some negative behaviors, we shouldn't be painting with such a broad brush.

Jessica missed out on years of women's ministry involvement and bonds because of her past and the stereotypical women's ministry she pictured—a bunch of boring older women sitting around tables with white linen tablecloths in the church fellowship hall, accomplishing nothing of substance. But in her thirties, her warped view of women's ministry shifted, and she slowly grew a heart for women. It didn't happen all at once.

First, God allowed her to fall in love with a group of women overseas. For years, her heart had been with the people of Rwanda, so it's fitting that the Lord used those Rwandan ladies to grow Jessica's passion for women. Eventually, her love overflowed into her church ministry. She also transitioned from youth pastor's wife to lead pastor's wife during this shift. In her new church, she dove right into leading the women's ministry (which previously would've been the last thing she'd ever choose to do on her own). As she got to know these women, she saw them as incredible, uniquely gifted friends. They weren't a bunch of petty people competing for position and status. Many of them were like-minded women who desired community too.

For those of you who relate to Jessica's younger days of irksome relationships, don't let your past friendships define what could be for your present community. God is a relational God. He created us so that He could have a relationship *with us*. He didn't intend for anybody to be alone, and He can build your community with the right people at the right time. Don't believe the lie that you're better off alone. God's Word confirms otherwise:

> Two people are better off than one, for they can help each other succeed. If one person falls, the other can reach out and help.

But someone who falls alone is in real trouble. Likewise, two people lying close together can keep each other warm. But how can one be warm alone? A person standing alone can be attacked and defeated, but two can stand back-to-back and conquer. Three are even better, for a triple-braided cord is not easily broken. (Eccles. 4:9–12)

Don't Be an Awkward Bobblehead

If there were a true polar opposite of Jessica and her aversion to female friendships, it would be Stephanie. This girl would befriend every gal she encountered if they'd let her. Whether introverted, extroverted, bookish, athletic, funny, or deadpan—no matter your personality or quirks—she would do whatever she could to draw you in as her new bestie. A friend once described her as a pitiful puppy who gets kicked away by its owner only to frolic right back to its abuser, tail wagging. She does whatever she can to reconcile relationships and, unfortunately, has been known to take an emotional beating or two along the way.

When Stephanie moved to their first church ministry in that tiny town in south Alabama, she was ready to mingle and forge lifelong friendships. Initially, her plan succeeded, but everything took a turn after she and Isaac began growing their family. With babies in tow, she felt isolated at home, unable to attend youth activities like she once could, and out of touch with the women her age who worked full-time jobs. As an over-the-top people person, she didn't know how to respond to the seclusion.

If you look up the definition of *overcompensate* in a digital dictionary, we're sure you'll find a headshot of Stephanie. When she realized friendships were growing distant, she pushed to pull them back (because that made total sense). And when other people formed bonds without her, she became one of those awkward bobblehead doll situations . . . you know, a plastic smile lurking in the vicinity of other people's conversations and relationships, not so discreetly waiting for her bobbing to be noticed.

The more city-girl Stephanie attempted to fit into the small-town mold, the more people misunderstood her. Some even avoided her, talked about her behind her back, and passive-aggressively uninvited her from their friend groups. It stung deeply. She spent many nights lying prostrate on her spit-up-stained carpet, soaked in tears as she begged God to show her what she had done wrong and how to make it right. Her prayer journal became her outlet as she pleaded with God to change hearts and asked Him to bless those who hurt her the most. She refused to grow bitter toward the people she loved, but her heart ached.

Stephanie isn't the only one who has faced loneliness in ministry despite desperately desiring friends. When you move away from home, following God into a new city and church (quite possibly a new state or country), there are definite roadblocks. You must start over, learning how the people in your church think and do life. There's a learning curve and sometimes a culture shock.

Those who have never moved away or served in church leadership before might be clueless about our struggle to make friends. Potential church friends may assume we're too busy to go out or must always have people inviting us to do things. But honestly, that's not usually the case. We could waste our time feeling sorry for ourselves, but what if we decided to make the first move instead, minus the bobblehead hovering?

When Stephanie and Isaac moved church homes (and cities) after more than a decade in that small town, Stephanie saw this move as an opportunity for a clean slate. She would be 100 percent herself whether people liked it or not. If some folks didn't care for her loud, quirky personality, she would let them be and find those who would embrace it. She didn't wait to be approached to make friends either. She bounced from person to person and table to table to introduce herself and began getting to know the people at her new church. Thankfully, she found women who embraced her. And she finally felt like she belonged.

It got even sweeter about two years in when a mutual friend introduced Stephanie to Jessica. Jess then turned around and introduced Stephanie to Jenna. A podcast, three matching tattoos, and a billion belly laughs later, we are best friends for life. The permanent ink sealed the deal.

This friendship didn't magically happen. It took intentionality and stepping outside our comfort zones with coffee dates and awkward phone conversations. Not every coffee date ends with matching tattoos, but you may never find your tribe if you wait for them to find you. You have to be the friend you want to find. Love people, see them, and listen to their stories as you hope someone else would do for you. As you do the groundwork of building a friendship, you'll find the ones who reciprocate. And for those who don't, you'll learn to walk away from them gracefully. Focus on the ones who do. No one needs a thousand friends. We need only a handful of real ones. Proverbs seems to agree: "A man of many companions may come to ruin, but there is a friend who sticks closer than a brother" (18:24 ESV).

You Can't Trust Everyone

One warning against pastors' wives and church leaders building friendships within their churches is that you never know whom you can trust. We would argue that this is the case for all relationships, no matter what you do for a living. We need to use wisdom and discernment to recognize who is trustworthy.

A few years ago, Jenna and Ian decided to join a parenting small group at their church. Jenna was hesitant about attending a small group because she felt like she didn't have the capacity for new friendships. She is an all-or-nothing gal, so she didn't want to join unless she could be all in. But she joined the group anyway, assuming she wouldn't get close with anyone but would participate in small group nights. She never expected the group to become so tight-knit they would go on vacations with one another.

On one of these getaways, as the whole group bonded and chatted, one individual voiced a few complaints about a particular ministry in their church. Jenna found it odd because she loved how that ministry ran. She had seen her fair share of shallow churches that essentially wrote that type of ministry off with fluff and surface-level teaching. Their church did things differently on purpose for a purpose. In response, she spoke positively about their church and didn't think much about the conversation.

Later, after returning home from this short trip, Jenna and Ian received a call about their small group conversation. Word had gotten back to the pastor about the vacation talk, except the facts were twisted. Jenna had been lumped in with the person who'd gossiped and complained about how the church functioned. Even though she had defended her church, simply listening and responding to this person's criticisms had affected her reputation. She knew right then that she needed to put up a healthy boundary. She still treated the gossiping person kindly and attended the same small group but avoided deep one-on-one conversations and friend dates. Jenna cringed when other people in the small group continued the attempt to build a close relationship with that person. But she kept her mouth shut, knowing that the truth always finds its way out.

Eventually, the rest of her small group friends started seeing the red flags without Jenna saying a word. (Quick sidebar: Let this remind us that we don't have to shout anyone else's sins from the rooftops. God will take care of it in time.) Because she set a boundary quietly, God protected her from the relational grenade that eventually exploded in the group, and she and her husband avoided the shrapnel.

As you can tell, we fully understand that some people don't belong in our inner circle. But no one has to fear befriending the wrong person if they listen closely to the Holy Spirit: "When the Spirit of truth comes, he will guide you into all truth. He will not speak on his own but will tell you what he has heard. He will tell you about the future" (John 16:13). Jenna believes God prompted her to put space between her and that individual. If she had ignored His guidance, she would have been hurt like her other friends were. We must tune in to the Lord's voice as we build new relationships.

How to Build Your Own Matching-Tattoos Community

Do you know what's annoying? When someone tells you to do something but doesn't leave you with any practical steps. We all know by now that community is vital, and we understand that we should be careful who fills that community. But simply saying it needs to be done doesn't magically *poof* healthy relationships into existence. We must be proactive. So here are a few ways we have learned to build our community.

First, we all subconsciously (or perhaps consciously) have formed expectations of what qualities would make a person the perfect friend for us. But sometimes, the best person for the season you're in is someone who is nothing like you pictured. You might need a friend older than you who can speak with confidence and candor about what they've learned over the years. Or you might benefit from a younger friend who is wise beyond her years and can bring energy back into the dead spaces of your life. You might need a quirky friend whose personality is not the type you usually gravitate to, or a got-it-mostly-together friend who has walked a tough road but made it out in one (scarred but mostly whole) piece. You could be surprised by who ends up making the best of friends. We know firsthand how beneficial it is to have friends in multiple age brackets and stages of life. We benefit from others with different life experiences.

Second, while longing for a friend, look for someone who needs one too. Amid writing this chapter, one of our kids opened up about not having friends at school. The best advice we could give him was to look for a lonely kid and sit with him. The next day, he noticed a boy in a different grade who sat alone at lunch and plopped down across the table from him. They officially became lunch pals, sitting with each other daily in the cafeteria. He could have ignored the advice and kept wallowing in his sadness, but instead he listened, and it panned out. The story's moral is this: see others if you want to be seen. Trust us: there is someone else seeking, just like you. Just pay attention. We all need each other.

Third, we cannot say it enough: proactivity is critical. Don't lounge around and wait for someone to invite you to the besties-for-life club. Take the initiative and ask a potential friend to coffee or, for those with little ones, on a playdate with your kids. We get that it can be awkward, especially for those of us with quieter, more introverted personalities. But stepping outside your comfort zone could pay off in incredible ways. It sure did for the three of us.

Fourth, another idea to help you find your tribe is to join a community Bible study or a small group outside your church. Stephanie traversed several years of loneliness in her former church. To find camaraderie, she joined a community Bible study group where she grew close with a pastor's wife at another local church. They spent time together weekly after Bible study. As a pastor's wife, this friend could relate to the pressures of church ministry life, which was a breath of fresh air for Stephanie. Don't underestimate the bonding power of a small, interest-driven group.

Fifth, we already hinted at our next piece of advice, but we'll put it in black and white: find other pastors' wives and ministry leaders to connect with in your area. More than likely, others nearby are searching for a community like you. If your husband has already met local pastors, ask him to invite his pastor acquaintances and their families over for dinner. Order pizza and keep it simple. (Or not! Five-course meals are acceptable if that's your jam. Also, could you drop us an invitation too?) If your hubby hasn't met any other pastors yet, perhaps you could take the initiative and facilitate a brunch/lunch for ministry leaders. Create cute invitations or purchase ready-made ones and pick a restaurant. Hand-deliver the invites to local churches or post them on social media. Never underestimate the power of social networking. We created a Facebook community group for pastors' wives and female pastors where members can interact and encourage each other. Many of them have met in person and are building friendships. Nobody gets what you are going through like another church leader!

Finally, the last piece of advice we want to leave you with is the most important. Pray for friends. It's the obvious step. But we get so focused on other people's conundrums and bigger messes within our own families we forget that God cares about the "little things" too. Jesus formed a thriving, tight-knit community with His disciples, so why wouldn't God desire the same for us? Be intentional and specific with your prayers; journal them if that works for you. Specific prayers get specific answers. We can attest that it's true. God has done it for us, and He can do it for you too.

The book of James gives us a perfect example:

If you need wisdom, ask our generous God, and he will give it to you. He will not rebuke you for asking. But when you ask him, be sure that your faith is in God alone. Do not waver, for a person with divided loyalty is as unsettled as a wave of the sea that is blown and tossed by the wind. Such people should not expect to receive anything from the Lord. Their loyalty is divided between God and the world, and they are unstable in everything they do. (1:5–8)

God's Word assures us that we will receive wisdom when we ask for it in faith. Confusion and misdirection wash away when we pray specifically for wisdom. We might not always like what God reveals to us, but we can be sure we will receive an answer. His Word promises us so. If we need wisdom in how to find true friendships that are mentally, emotionally, and spiritually healthy, we can ask for it, and God will lead the way as He promises.

Stop aimlessly wandering the middle school lunchroom aisles. There is a seat at the table for you. You might have to dodge a few mush-faced mishaps and endure some awkward conversations, but you will find your people. And ministry life will be that much sweeter because of it.

11

The Pastor's Wife
Pastors Too

> Women don't need to find a voice, they have a voice, and they need to feel empowered to use it, and people need to be encouraged to listen.
>
> —Meghan Markle

Jelly is underrated. It follows peanut butter in the classic peanut butter *and* jelly sandwich, after all. And this is coming from women who lionize peanut butter. Case in point, Stephanie's obsession with seasonal Reese's peanut butter cups. What makes these Reese's eggs, Christmas trees, hearts, pumpkins, and more so delectable is the ample amount of peanut butter in their chocolate-to-peanut-butter ratio—pure heaven on earth. So please don't take it lightly when we say that jelly is underrated. Nobody adores peanut butter as much as we do. But we cannot forget that jelly brings sweetness to the savory.

It enhances the sandwich experience while containing the ability to stand alone on a delightful English muffin. And a homemade jelly that has been preserved straight from the vine? Our mouths are watering. Jelly is a standout condiment that amplifies other condiments *and* can hold its own.

Being a pastor's wife is like the jelly on a peanut butter and jelly sandwich. We can easily get forgotten among all the peanut butter rage. We get it. Peanut butter (aka our pastor spouses) is incredible. We are their biggest fans. But like jelly, we also bring an abundance of worth to the table. *Pun intended.*

Not all pastors' spouses are the same. Some are highly involved in day-to-day church ministry responsibilities. Others take more of a backseat, focusing on their children, home life, or other work. And some fall somewhere in between. It's a spectrum. But no matter where we land on it, we all pastor alongside our spouses somehow.

The Job You Do for Zero Pay

While discussing the direction of this chapter, Jessica multitasked like a pro. She handled the laundry; set up childcare so one of their ministries could run efficiently; scheduled meetings; worked on her nonprofit, Come Away Missions; and booked tickets for a mission trip to Africa. And oops, the dog relieved herself on the carpet among the chaos, so she cleaned up urine too. And between nonprofit work and dog pee, Jessica counseled a tearful woman while quietly enduring a difficult season in her own personal life. She doesn't receive a paycheck for any of it, yet she serves regardless—with most people oblivious to the chaos behind the scenes. Many pastors' spouses do the same.

In some churches, the pastor's wife is expected to run the women's or children's ministry, counsel women, and manage the home efficiently so her husband can focus on his pastoral duties, *all without compensation*. Isn't this odd, when you think about it? But no one expects anything different. What other field expects an individual to do the same things their spouse does as a job without pay?

We understand that we are called to church ministry alongside our husbands. We honestly wouldn't want to be anywhere else or doing anything else but the twenty things we're juggling right now. As hard as it is, and despite receiving minimal recognition and zero compensation, we are called, too, and we know God will take care of us. He will reward us. He sees every sacrifice and service we provide our church community, even when others miss it. We do none of this for the approval of other people. We do it for the approval of God: "Work willingly at whatever you do, as though you were working for the Lord rather than for people. Remember that the Lord will give you an inheritance as your reward, and that the Master you are serving is Christ" (Col. 3:23–24). On difficult days, we remember our why. We could demand acknowledgment and payment for meeting the expectations and fulfilling the church responsibilities, but we know where our ultimate reward comes from.

The Ultimate Empaths

Jenna and Jessica both own goldendoodles that act like humans. These dogs will cut their eyes at you, huff when they don't get their way, and wrap their paws around you while standing on their hind legs for the cuddliest bear hugs. They are exceptional pets. We wonder if God created animals with this much personality because He knew we would need those furry snuggles on hard days.

Stephanie has never owned a goldendoodle, but she and Isaac adopted two endearing mutts, Roxie and Reese, early in their marriage. These cuties were Stephanie's babies. She didn't have people babies yet, but these furry ones kept her occupied and brought so much joy. The only downfall to building a bond with her dogs was losing them. Roxie went first, and Stephanie mourned her pup for months while cuddling nightly with Reese as tears trickled down her cheeks. While she grieved, she noticed something different about Reese. Her lone fur baby was distraught. She would aimlessly wander the house and yard as if searching for something. And at night, when Stephanie could not sleep, Reese seemed to understand her sadness. They both remained solemn as the minutes ticked by in the silent darkness. We wonder if dogs are true empaths. Their connection to their owners and other pets in the home gives us reason to believe it's possible.

Stephanie is a lot like her sweet pup, minus the propensity for begging for food with her tongue flapping in the wind. (Well, begging, yes. Tongue flapping, we hope not.) She gets attached to family, friends, and pets easily. And the bond she shares with her husband and kids is fierce. When Stephanie would overhear a church member complaining about Isaac or when gossip about her hubby got back to her, it took everything in her power not to scream and hurl things like a hangry preschooler. And the only time she ever saw tears well up in Isaac's eyes because of a false accusation, she came unglued. No one messes with her hubby: *no one.* The burdens her husband carried—she felt the weight of them too. The pain he endured felt magnified within her.

Work is rarely left at "work." Pastors continue to bear the emotional and mental weight of their jobs when they leave the church office. Sometimes the burdens become too great, and they break, leaving their spouses to pick up the pieces. Pastors' wives uplift our husbands when the unthinkable happens. When slander wrecks his name, a close staff member chooses to go, or the enemy pushes him to give up, we are there, encouraging him and mourning with him as he faces every hardship. In a sense, we pastor the pastor. We call him out when he's wrong. We comfort him in sadness. We cheer for him when he walks boldly in his calling. We even take off our earrings and go to bat for him when he gets mistreated. We do so much more behind closed doors than people realize, and we strive to honor Proverbs 31: "Her husband can trust her, and she will greatly enrich his life. She brings him good, not harm, all the days of her life" (vv. 11–12).

When You Didn't Pick This Life

This might surprise you, but Jenna did not marry a pastor. Ian was an elementary school teacher for the first part of their marriage. So, when he informed her that God had asked him to quit his stable, insurance-providing job to step into full-time ministry, Jenna considered whacking him upside the head. (We kid, we kid.) She only panicked for one excruciatingly long minute and then went straight to God. By the following day, she had peace with her husband moving forward into this calling (the key word being *husband*).

While Stephanie and Jessica felt called to serve in church ministry, Jenna did not. She did feel called to support Ian but struggled to understand where she fit or what role she played at church. She only knew God called her and their family to walk alongside her husband. While some pastors' wives mentor other women and counsel children and teens, Jenna focused on her babies and home.

You might relate to Jenna. How you "pastor" differs from others, but what you do is still vital. When pastors have support and help at home, they can thrive . . . because let's get real, it's refreshing for someone to have your back after you've had everyone else's backs all day, every day.

You could be in a season when your focus must be entirely on your home, which is completely okay, but you also need to address the possibility that fear is holding you back from your calling. Some should be serving in the church with their spouses but allow insecurities or confusion to halt their efforts. They have gifts, yet they squander them.

As time passed and her babies grew, something else kept Jenna from being active in the ministry. Insecure and confusing thoughts filled her mind often. She never planned to be a pastor's wife, so she never sought counsel on how she could be an integral part of Ian's ministry. Conversely, nobody noticed her newbie vibes and asked how they could help her step into a more active role. We believe there should be more of us "seasoned" pastors' wives teaching the newer ones. And not in an *I know better than you, so listen to me* way but a concerned *I know what you're going through* way.

It hasn't been until the last few years that Jenna has found space to serve. She is passionate about photography but never thought taking pictures would be a skill she could utilize in ministry. She and Ian attend a multisite church with "dream teams" (groups that church members can join and serve within). One team, the creative team, consisted of members with a knack for photography. They would capture baptisms, worship, and other sweet moments of their church people on camera and, through these snapshots, share what God was doing with His people. But during COVID lockdowns, this team disbanded.

Even though the creative team had become nonexistent, Jenna noticed one woman at their church site taking baptism pictures every month. She wondered if she could help, but at first she squashed any interest stirring within her to use her photography skills with the assumption that the church had it handled. They were a megachurch, after all. Why would they need her help? Though she had doubts, eventually she did ask if the church had room for a second photographer. And lo and behold, they did need one! The next thing she knew, Jenna became the person behind the lens. This new position breathed life into her. At first she shared her photography duties, but the original photographer slowly stepped away from the camera to serve in the children's ministry, leaving Jenna as the sole photographer.

As the various teams began to come back after COVID, the assistant pastor contacted Jenna, inquiring if she would be interested in officially serving on the creative team. The lady leading the team at the main church campus had reached out to all the assistant pastors to see if any photographers at their locations would be a good fit for the team. Jenna accepted gladly.

Since the creative team was based out of the main campus and she was the sole photographer on her campus, Jenna didn't have team members to serve alongside. She wanted to be a part of a real "team." But her church had an interview process, and she didn't want to overstep. Where could she find creatives wishing to grow with her and use their talents to serve the church, and how could she make it happen?

Sometimes we get tunnel vision. We see only one way to do things—our way. We forget that it's not up to us to make things happen when God lays an assignment in our laps. Jenna realized she hadn't stopped to ask God to bring her teammates. If she wanted to build a team, she needed His eyes, so she prayed for God to place the right people in her path. And He showed out.

One day, as Jenna was snapping pictures at another church event, a woman approached her to ask if she could help take photographs. Jenna perked up, realizing God had answered her prayer and brought a fellow creative to her. Excitedly, she discussed an idea with her pastor that had been stirring within her for people, like this lady, who desired to serve in the creative space. Her pastor gave her the green light, so a small group specifically for creatives was born. Instead of her husband being the one leading, she was the one shepherding.

Two creatives who adored photography as much as Jenna did joined the group. She mentored them and checked in on them often. One of these women had gone through the wringer. As a single mom, her load was heavy. Jenna wondered if she would stick with the creative group for the long run, but this resilient lady surprised her. She officially joined the creative team and faithfully served.

Seeing this woman's transformation was powerful. Jenna has always known that God can change people, and she had seen it happen through Ian's ministry. But this time, He used her. Despite her insecurities and confusion about her place in the church, God brought Jenna a group of women she could pour into. Her obedience to God's leading changed her life.

If you know you should be doing more but are allowing fear to undermine God's leading, reach out to a trusted counselor and explore whatever could be below the surface, keeping you from stepping fully into your ministry. The church doesn't only need the pastor. It benefits from your touch too. Let's trash the baggage and run our race:

> Therefore, since we are surrounded by such a huge crowd of witnesses to the life of faith, let us strip off every weight that slows us down, especially the sin that so easily trips us up. And let us run with endurance the race God has set before us. We do this by keeping our eyes on Jesus, the champion who initiates and perfects our faith. Because of the joy awaiting him, he endured the cross, disregarding its shame. Now he is seated in the place of honor beside God's throne. (Heb. 12:1–2)

Embrace Your Jelly

No matter how difficult church life can be. No matter how grueling the demands of ministry can get. No matter how ugly it becomes behind the scenes, there is nothing else in this world we would rather do. Being there for a couple as they make plans to tie the knot and getting honest with them about both the good and the hard of marriage is rewarding in ways we can't explain. When someone's blind eyes are finally opened, and they experience a God-sized breakthrough, we revel in their freedom. When our husbands preach a message that speaks directly to our hearts, not just the rest of the congregation, we well up with pride . . . not the lofty kind, but the kind of pride where we feel ridiculously blessed to be married to a man who lives what he preaches. Seeing transformation and the movement of the Holy Spirit makes it all worth it. We really can rejoice always: "Always be full of joy in the Lord. I say it again—rejoice!" (Phil. 4:4). And no one can steal our joy: "So you have sorrow now, but I will see you again; then you will rejoice, and no one can rob you of that joy" (John 16:22).

Church friends, can we ask you for your help? Please, recognize the load your pastor's spouse bears. Know that we pastor behind the scenes too. We wrestle mentally, emotionally, and spiritually with all the ministry things as well. There is no Off button. (But wouldn't that be fabulous? Somebody sign us up for the button that sends us on a tropical vacation with zero emergency phone calls. That sounds fun.)

Remember that we live for the moments when we can help you, but it's fantastic when you check in on us too. We have gotten exceptional at concealing our messes, but trust us: they are there. We can't take a mental health day . . . or can we? We should look into that!

Here's the point: when we have a terrible day, we need a safe place to land. We need a morale boost to avoid burnout after a string of emotionally exhausting church catastrophes. Church leaders are not superheroes. We are the first responders who also need saving while doing our part to help the bystanders in our vicinity.

For the pastors' spouses who are feeling like abandoned jelly, don't stop. Keep serving. Keep loving. Keep doing the work God called *you* to do. Your pastoring matters; the church would be bland without your rich and abundant flavor.

12

~~~

The Pastor's Wife
Gets Hurt by the Church Too

Christ bears the wounds of the church, his body, just as he bore the wounds of crucifixion. I sometimes wonder which have hurt worse.

—Philip Yancey

When Stephanie was six years old, she didn't have many friends. Other kids failed to see the charm of her incessant chatter and thunderous attempts to fit in with her class. First graders can be savage. One lonely afternoon on the school playground, Stephanie lounged beneath a tree while waiting her turn to swing. She was daydreaming (as she was prone to do when she wasn't blabbering on and on to any poor soul in her vicinity) while she lingered near the swing set.

Finally, a swing came available, and she darted to occupy it. However, Stephanie's euphoria over swaying back and forth through the breeze was short-lived because her teacher summoned her before she could fully bask in her triumph. As Stephanie neared her teacher, she detected a swarm of first-grade girls huddled around a tearful friend. The little girl sniffled and smudged giant teardrops on her cheeks while the teacher peered directly into Stephanie's eyes and began a swift interrogation: "Did you push _____ off the swing?"

Stephanie's mouth dropped open as she quickly answered with a shaky no. She hadn't pushed anybody, but one of the students comforting the tearful girl claimed she had seen the whole thing. *Stephanie shoved her right off the swing so she could take a turn* . . . only she hadn't. The accusatory child had lied many times before, but Stephanie seemed to be the only one not experiencing a bout of amnesia. She insisted she hadn't shoved anyone, but the teacher reprimanded her for lying and sent her to the principal's office. Her principal told her she would not leave the office until she admitted to pushing her classmate. Eventually, after telling the truth a hundred times, Stephanie did precisely what everyone accused her of doing—she lied. She confessed to doing something she didn't do and invited guilt and fear into a place they should never have been in the first place.

She was only a child when this happened, but it impacted her deeply. As an adult, she still fears being falsely accused of wrongdoing and losing relationships. If a lie this small from years ago can wound a person for years to come, how much more can lies, manipulation, slander, and gossip from a church member affect a person today?

More and more people are sharing stories of trauma they have faced in the church. Scroll for a few minutes on social media, and you'll come across at least one of these hot topics: spiritual abuse, manipulation, and church hurt. The sad truth is that these are more than buzzwords; these are real problems.

When Church Hurt *Hurts*

For centuries, Bible verses have been used as weapons in the church. Whether it's an unhealthy pastor covering up wrong-doing or church members expecting a church leader to receive church hurt in silence, pastors and church members have misused Scripture. Take these verses in Matthew 5, for example:

> You have heard the law that says the punishment must match the injury: "An eye for an eye, and a tooth for a tooth." But I say, do not resist an evil person! If someone slaps you on the right cheek, offer the other cheek also. If you are sued in court and your shirt is taken from you, give your coat, too. (vv. 38–40)

Too many people encourage victims of abuse to stay silent, to "turn the other cheek," while allowing the abuser to go unscathed for the sake of the church's reputation. They prioritize saving face over saving victims.

The church has gotten good at gaslighting its members and its leaders when problems arise. What is corrupt is concealed with a veil of phony niceties and plastic smiles. When we cover up the messy truth, darkness spreads unchecked. And we are left with a suffering, unproductive church body. Pretending you're unhurt doesn't make it so. It's like placing a Mickey Mouse bandage on a festering bullet wound. We know how it feels because we've been the wounded ones flaunting our cartoonish dressings.

Jessica has faced church hurt more than once. She witnessed church leaders living in flagrant sin without consequence and learned early on that there were pastors who preached on stage weekly yet lived a lifestyle contrary to their sermons. Some pastors were utterly broken.

Jessica's heart steeped in anger the more aware she became of the corruption surrounding her. In one church where she and Jonathan served as youth pastors early on in their marriage, they received their first real taste of church hurt. They lived there for only six months but faced hell on earth almost immediately. Not just one but *three* literal hurricanes tore through and around their city. Jonathan's mother grew ill with the sickness that would eventually take her life. And to top it all off, she and Jonathan felt like outsiders in their church family. She recalls church staff members mocking their Southern accents while the lead pastor barely even spoke to them. The loneliness was all-consuming. Uprooting their lives to move to a place they would call home for less than a year felt like a waste. But we have learned that God wastes nothing.

As they plodded on, they had no idea they were learning lessons (the "what-not-to-dos") they would use down the road as lead pastors. And they decided that if they ever pastored their own church, it would be different. They would build intimacy among the church staff, teaching them how to encourage and serve one another through their actions. Nobody could blatantly sin without being called out and called up to Jesus. They would bring everything to the light as Ephesians teaches:

> Take no part in the worthless deeds of evil and darkness; instead, expose them. It is shameful even to talk about the things that ungodly people do in secret. But their evil intentions will be exposed when the light shines on them, for the light makes everything visible. This is why it is said,
>
> > "Awake, O sleeper,
> > rise up from the dead,
> > and Christ will give you light." (5:11–14)

The church hurt didn't end after this six-month stint. The following two churches would bring their fair share of anger and tears too. Seeming to be a wolf in sheep's clothing in Jessica's mind, the pastor they served under during this period played the part of a faithful shepherd effortlessly from the stage while disparaging Jessica and Jonathan behind closed doors. He would take jabs at Jonathan often, even telling him he wasn't a "real" pastor, "just" a youth minister.

Leaders in the church attempted to block Jessica from serving in Rwanda, where God had called her to do mission work. She was confounded about how any Christian could purposely halt people from following their God-sized callings. But the Lord reminded her of the apostle Paul. The world didn't try to block him as he went on his missionary journeys—the religious groups did.

> Then the Jews stirred up the influential religious women and the leaders of the city, and they incited a mob against Paul and Barnabas and ran them out of town. (Acts 13:50)

> But Jews came from Antioch and Iconium, and having persuaded the crowds, they stoned Paul and dragged him out of the city, supposing that he was dead. (14:19 ESV)

> While Gallio was proconsul of Achaia, the Jews made a united attack against Paul and brought him to the tribunal. (18:12 CSB)

Sadly, we can sometimes be in the same situation when those who are supposed to be our faithful teammates turn against us.

While their pastor mistreated them, Jessica had to show up on Sundays smiling and listen to the man in the pulpit who was striving to ruin her ministry. She would scan the crowd in the pews and wonder how these people didn't recognize the corruption standing before their eyes. How could they not see the wool costume draped over this wolf?

If Jessica and Jonathan knew then what they know now, they might have run when red flags started popping up here and there and *everywhere* . . . like a bad Dr. Seuss rhyme. Later they learned that their pastor and a handful of personnel members had held private meetings where they schemed how to get rid of Jessica and Jonathan without the rest of the church's knowledge. In the end, they were unjustly fired. The icing on the cake came in the form of a nondisclosure agreement they were told to sign if they wanted to receive a full severance package—an offer they literally couldn't refuse because they were smack dab in the middle of an expensive adoption to bring their baby girl home from China. The pastor lied to the church from the pulpit about why Jessica and Jonathan left, and they couldn't tell anyone the truth at the time.

Jessica was furious. The anger consumed her every time she ran into one of the people who'd hurt her, while they acted as if nothing had happened. Her indignation bubbled over each time her daily trek took her along the road from which she would see the church building. And when she remembered how hard her husband had worked to grow the youth group spiritually and numerically, and did so quite successfully, she imagined burning houses to the ground. (Don't worry, she never acted out her colorful imagination! No pyromaniacs here.)

Whenever Jessica dreamed of taking matters into her own hands, the Holy Spirit's voice would get loud. He would fight this battle for her. She didn't have to do a thing, because the truth always came to light. She needed to be still and watch the show, and a verse in Exodus became her solace: "The LORD will fight for you; you need only to be still" (14:14 NIV).

Jessica could hear the Lord say to her, *Child, simmer down. I've got you. I've got your husband. I've got your children. I've got your life.* He likes to speak real direct-like to His hot-headed daughter. She listened. And she tried to forgive, knowing she would never be in a right relationship with God if she refused obedience in forgiveness.

So if you are presenting a sacrifice at the altar in the Temple and you suddenly remember that someone has something against you, leave your sacrifice there at the altar. Go and be reconciled to that person. Then come and offer your sacrifice to God. (Matt. 5:23–24)

Forgiveness is a must, but it can sometimes be tricky. Jessica would think she had finally forgiven these people, but then she would be rudely awakened to the unforgiveness simmering beneath her surface when any of their names were brought up in conversation. Out of sight, they were out of her mind. But when she saw them or heard about them, her anger would begin to stir. It took a solid year for her to be able to truly forgive them. She had to deal with her heart issue in order to be fully free from her bitter, burning-houses-down root of unforgiveness. Peace came only when she committed all of the hurt and anger to her God, who was far more capable of handling it all.

Confrontation Is Not a Dirty Word

If you haven't figured it out yet, we believe everything done in the dark should be brought to light. When one of us is hurt by another, we talk it out. If food particles lodge themselves into awkward places, like front teeth or shirt crevices, we point it out (Are you friends if you don't?). When anxious thoughts or depression creeps in, we call it what it is. This is what real friends do. But it shouldn't only be friends who bring things to light. We should always bring light to the darkness.

Jenna is not naturally confrontational. She would rather cut her entire lawn with a dull pair of kindergarten scissors than face people who have wronged her or hurt her feelings. She'll use her acting skills all day long, every single day, before giving in to having an awkward conversation. But several years ago, she faced a situation she couldn't ignore.

Jenna's husband had been serving as a youth pastor for a time but knew he needed to step down to follow God's leading. He gave more than a year's notice (exceptionally longer than the polite two weeks most people offer in secular job positions). They didn't want to leave the youth group and church without setting them up for future success. Jenna's husband buckled down and poured his focus into discipleship, something every church leader should strive to do. Over that last year, the church showed no interest in looking for someone to fill Ian's shoes when he and Jenna eventually left. They had plenty of time, but they did zero searching.

One person stirred the pot, even though Jenna and Ian believed they were leaving on good terms. Gossip is always frustrating, but when a leader in the church spreads the gossip, it's damaging. This individual grumbled about Ian "leaving the church in a mess," blaming problems on him that he had nothing to do with and slandering his character.

Jenna, the girl who detests confrontation, stood up for her husband and broke their silence. She knew if this pastor would lie in this scenario, he could do it again to someone else. Jenna turned her hurt and anger into productive action. She wrote a letter to the lead pastor, expressing her irritation and revealing the deception in the church staff.

We hear the hushed gasps coming from the other side of this book. We get it if you're shocked and appalled at Jenna's response. We have all been taught to endure "persecution," to roll over when unhealthy people harm us with their thoughtless words and actions. But in our attempt to "do the right thing" and be "the bigger person," we have taught bullies, manipulators, and narcissists that boundaries don't matter. They can continue leading in our spiritual circles while pushing people away from the church. And no one will do a single thing about it.

When we choose to avoid confrontation and refuse to bring everything hidden behind closed doors to the light, we become the problem. Scripture is clear on this matter:

> Thieves break into houses at night
>   and sleep in the daytime.
> They are not acquainted with the light. (Job 24:16)

This is the verdict: Light has come into the world, but people loved darkness instead of light because their deeds were evil. Everyone who does evil hates the light, and will not come into the light for fear that their deeds will be exposed. But whoever lives by the truth comes into the light, so that it may be seen plainly that what they have done has been done in the sight of God. (John 3:19–21 NIV)

Darkness should never be allowed to spread unchecked. As members of the "big C" church, we are responsible for setting healthy boundaries and following through with church discipline when necessary. The pedestals must be torn down. And the Lord will light our way.

> Do not gloat over me, my enemies!
>   For though I fall, I will rise again.
> Though I sit in darkness,
>   the Lord will be my light. (Mic. 7:8)

Jenna's letter did receive a relatively good response. The lead pastor assured them he would handle the person spreading the gossip and apologized for the hurt they experienced. She doesn't know if he ever followed through with what he said he would do, but she learned that she could use her voice and find strength even if she had to stand alone in her defense of the truth.

When any of us discover that others are gossiping or spreading slander about us, we can be brave enough to approach the person hurting us, especially if we are tempted to gossip and slander in return. Sometimes restoration can come only if we make the first move. But if restoration still doesn't come, we can rest in doing the right thing, even when it's hard. God sees us, and that's all that matters.

When FOMO Breeds Church Hurt

For years Stephanie was an avid runner. Nearly every afternoon, after Isaac came home from work, she would slide on her tennis shoes and jog up and down the streets of her small town. Along the way, she signed up for a few 5Ks and competed against herself for a better time each race. Running was exhilarating.

One of the 5Ks she participated in was a mud run hosted by a local camp. Stephanie was pumped to sign up, especially when multiple other women from her church also decided to participate. A few of these women were friends she had lately felt distant from, so she thought this would be the perfect opportunity to spend time with them. She didn't realize it would have the total opposite effect.

When Stephanie asked these girls to tell her when they were available to run and train together, the response was crickets. She continued to train with two other ladies in her church, and sometimes alone when they could not join her. The situation became more emotional one day when she scrolled through Instagram and saw that the girls she wanted to practice with had posted pictures of running together. Her heart hurt.

Race day came, and Stephanie forced herself to participate with a smile despite her complicated emotions. She enjoyed spending time with the other church ladies who'd trained with her, but she choked back tears when her former friends arrived. They were wearing matching race-day shirts. If FOMO (aka *fear of missing out*) was a person, he might as well have body-slammed Stephanie to the muddy ground. Here she was, a youth pastor's wife in a town where she had zero family members nearby, and the friends she'd once spent time with like they were family looked better off without her.

This type of church hurt digs deep. It's complicated because no one outright sinned or said anything cruel directly to her face. She didn't know what she had done to push these friends away, but she convinced herself the problem must be her. She was sure she had hurt someone in that group and needed to make it right. But the damage would never be fully reversed.

Trouble comes when we strive to fix something that can't be repaired. Many church leaders have been hurt in this same manner, constantly feeling like outsiders and not fitting in no matter what they do. It's like high school drama *on steroids*.

––––––––

Church, we want you to know that we fight loneliness too. We are real people who desire closure and restoration when there is a relationship rift. We are hurt more often than anyone realizes, even when the wound is inflicted unintentionally.

Looking back, Stephanie wishes she had brought more of this rift to the light. She should have been honest and moved on if these friends wanted space. But she decided not to address it. She pushed back the aching until it was a dull gnawing. And eventually, her silent cries came to a head. When she moved to a new town, anxiety attacks and physical ailments plagued her as her fear of making friends only to lose them took root. Unresolved church hurt almost always leads to deep wounds.

Church hurt must be dealt with, big or small. Most of the time, the small things are more significant than we realize. Trauma takes many forms and will suffocate those who choose to ignore it. Change must happen.

When we are hurt by the church, we can move on only if we choose to face the hurt. We shouldn't ignore it. And we shouldn't wallow in it. A happy medium exists where we acknowledge the hurt, seek reconciliation, and move on with the help of God and perhaps a mentor (or therapist). Seek help. Pray earnestly. Forgive and move forward.

Like Stephanie on that fateful day at the schoolyard swing set, we will experience church hurt. We will be responsible for calling out spiritual abuse. Emotions are sure to get the best of us now and again. But we can be healthy leaders in a thriving church body who become more robust and wiser on the other side of church hurt.

And for all you spirited types like Jessica, please step away from the matches. Burning down houses is never the answer.

13

~~~~~

The Pastor's Wife
Gets Angry and Annoyed with the Church Too

Usually when people are sad, they don't do anything. They just cry over their condition. But when they get angry, they bring about a change.

—Malcolm X

Parenting does something to a person. The one who was once as oozingly sweet as freshly whipped buttercream icing morphs into a ruthless despot. "Touch that blazing stovetop, I dare you. That's what you get for being hardheaded!" We can become merciless. Tough love is our love language, or at least that's what we tell ourselves.

Yes, we were once the judgy bystanders in the grocery store parking lot witnessing a toddler tantrum turned epic show-down between a strong-willed child and a headstrong parent.

Our eyebrows raised in disbelief, and our heads shook as we envisioned how differently our children would act in public and how calmly we would respond to their disobedience. But we eventually became parents, and our eyes were jerked wide open to the complexities of parenting. It's a jungle out there, folks.

As we ponder how fiddly raising children can be, we see some similarities between the emotions attached to becoming a church leader and the emotions in parenting. It's easy to be the one on the outside looking in, telling people how they should act or feel, but it's entirely different when you are the one living this complex and multifaceted life. The emotions are messy, and sometimes those big feelings explode out of us, shocking everyone around us, including ourselves. Just because you're a pastor's wife doesn't mean you inherit cool, calm, and collected genes. You get angry too.

As pastors' wives, we have been taught to bottle our anger, to have a tender heart and tough skin, and to accept the reality that church hurts sometimes. But we aren't emotionless androids able to withstand hurt feelings and righteous (or not-so-righteous) anger. We get angry. We grow bitter, though we know God warns against it: "And 'don't sin by letting anger control you.' Don't let the sun go down while you are still angry" (Eph. 4:26). We have nearly drowned in the waves of our sorrow and a mountain of Culver's frozen custard (don't knock it until you try it), all the while concealing our knotted-up emotions because that's what people in ministry are *supposed to do.*

We are exhausted from pretending and are moving on to healthier ways of coping with our feisty feelings.

How Nostalgia Hurts the Church

Holiday traditions are fun. The annual beach trip Jenna's family takes every summer. The loaded hot chocolate doused with clouds of whipped cream, sprinkles, caramel, and chocolate syrup drizzles that Jessica's family enjoys all Christmas. The Black Friday, er . . . Thursday(ish) shopping spree Stephanie schemes for every Thanksgiving. And the pool parties we throw every spring and summer. These traditions are grounded in sweet nostalgia and feel-good endorphins. They fill us with Neverland-type thoughts of never growing up (and a few extra pounds). But sometimes traditions can become security blankets we fall back on when what we really need is to reassess if they are truly helpful or a hindrance.

When one of Stephanie's children was seven months old, he struggled to fall asleep. Every night like clockwork, his doughy little body would vociferously toss and turn as he squalled in a panic. It took a few nights for Stephanie to realize he might be afraid of being alone in his dark room. Stephanie comforted her little guy by plugging a night light into the wall and offering him a small blue stuffed puppy someone had bestowed as a gift. As she tucked the squishy toy next to her son, his cries quieted. This night started ten years of the blue puppy named Puppy (they are super original in the Gilbert household) being an adopted member of the family. It was her son's security blanket, so sleep was impossible without Puppy. If it was missing, the world paused while the troops searched their vicinity until they retrieved the missing family member.

Over the years, Puppy faded to a dull gray, and a tiny opening on his threadbare nose, barely noticeable at first, began to expand. Even after repairing that hole, before long a new tear would open, and stuffing would peek out from a new rip in his nose or neck. When Stephanie's son was ten, the wear and tear on Puppy's face and neck had nearly decapitated it. Since the Gilberts aren't fans of beheading, Stephanie had to convince her son to retire Puppy to a shelf where it could live out its final raggedy years. This was no easy feat. Her son adored his Puppy and relied on it for peaceful sleep. He clung to Puppy like grass stains on a white T-shirt. The process of letting go was draining.

Even though traditions can be a positive experience, some church traditions are like the stuffed puppy that brought comfort and purpose in its time but desperately needs to be shelved before any heads are lost. We are in trouble if we cling to a policy or event because "it's always been this way" or because nostalgia has blinded us to the dilapidated mess before us.

Jenna and Ian served in a church steeped in tradition. The congregation had rules, and these rules were meant to be followed. Case in point: they always observed communion after every church service. And the pastor blessed said communion *every* time they served it. One Sunday when the pastor traveled out of town, Ian preached the Sunday morning sermon after leading worship as usual during the service. Now, Ian was not officially ordained. He preached, taught, and led worship regularly, but the church considered him a layperson, not a minister. Since the pastor was unavailable to bless the Lord's Supper, Ian could not administer communion. He could preach. He could lead in the church. But without the correct documents, he could not "bless" the Lord's Supper. This tradition was so deeply ingrained in the church that the church even prohibited Ian from having communion with the teens he led at camp without the proper blessing. He had to video call the pastor to bless the communion . . . virtually.

Jenna and Ian would make light of this absurdity with passive-aggressive jokes to each other in the privacy of their home, but Jenna seethed on the inside. None of this made sense to her. Even church members and leadership didn't understand why they served communion in this manner. It had just always been done that way. Despite her annoyance, Jenna and Ian kept the anger contained and never stirred the pot. But to this day, they are hyperaware of such unhealthy traditions and avoid them like the bubonic plague.

The comparison between some church traditions and the traditions of the Pharisees is too eerily similar. The Gospel of Mark recounts a time when some religious leaders set out to question Jesus about observing traditions:

(The Jews, especially the Pharisees, do not eat until they have poured water over their cupped hands, as required by their ancient traditions. Similarly, they don't eat anything from the market until they immerse their hands in water. This is but one of many traditions they have clung to—such as their ceremonial washing of cups, pitchers, and kettles.)

So the Pharisees and teachers of religious law asked him, "Why don't your disciples follow our age-old tradition? They eat without first performing the hand-washing ceremony."

Jesus replied, "You hypocrites! Isaiah was right when he prophesied about you, for he wrote,

'These people honor me with their lips,
but their hearts are far from me.
Their worship is a farce,
for they teach man-made ideas as commands from God.'"
(7:3–7)

The religious leaders of Jesus's day added many rules to God's law. They confused human traditions with the law of God, and Jesus reprimanded them. In our current-day churches, we too easily become like the Pharisees, making up our own rules based on tradition. If doing this was wrong in Jesus's time, it's still wrong today.

Don't Be a Hoarder

Back in the pre–Netflix binging days, TLC shows were all the rage, at least in Stephanie's home. *What Not to Wear* and

Say Yes to the Dress were clear favorites. (How could they not be? And all the millennial '80s babies collectively nod in agreement.)

TLC was known for feel-good stories with feel-great endings. But one show's spine-chilling scenes would send any germophobe into cardiac arrest and perhaps a straitjacket. *Hoarding: Buried Alive* mesmerized Stephanie. How could anyone collect so much clutter and garbage? The answer always had psychological roots. Most stayed in the pit of their trauma, collecting things to cover old wounds until they made their homes unlivable.

Sadly, some churches are chained to this same scarcity mentality. They hoard financial resources when God's Word teaches a *wealth* of generosity. (See what we did there?) Christians and the church as a whole should be noted for our giving hearts. When a church sits on hundreds of thousands—even millions—of dollars in the bank, there's a problem.

Jenna saw firsthand how greedy church people could be. At that communion stickler of a church, their bank account could have taken every single homeless person off the streets of their small town. Heck, it could have built a freaking mansion to give shelter to the unhoused. But there the money sat, rotting behind steel like a forgotten month-old banana.

In that wealthy church, a lady faithfully served, giving her time and resources without complaint as she raised four children alone while her husband served in the military. One time when her husband was away, her refrigerator expired, leaving her unable to store food for her four growing kids. Ian informed the church staff of this lady's need and asked if the church had a benevolence fund they could pull from to help her. Mind you: this church could fill a warehouse slap full of refrigerators. But the answer Ian received was no. That's it. The church allocated no money to help people like this woman. Ian and a few other youth leaders ended up banding together to purchase, deliver, and install a refrigerator for this family.

Despite this church's hesitation to spend its nest egg on individuals in need, they were quick to spend ungodly amounts of cash on sprucing up the church building and pressure washing the parking lot. The church was dying on the inside, but the walls were sparkling. Every year when the church discussed funds, they would cheer and clap when informed of the millions of dollars filling their precious endowment fund. And not long after Jenna and Ian ended their time serving there, they heard a story that made them come unglued. Supposedly, a dear old saint had gone home to be with her Savior and left her worldly lot, equaling a whopping $2 million, to none other than the church's endowment fund. *Of course.*

Americanized churches have failed to reproduce the core tenets of the New Testament church. Instead of giving whatever resources we own to help others who lack in our church family, we greedily hoard in fear of losing our immaculate buildings. Never mind the people—the actual church. It saddens us almost as much as it angers us to see how far off course we've strayed from the early church:

> And all the believers met together in one place and shared everything they had. They sold their property and possessions and shared the money with those in need. They worshiped together at the Temple each day, met in homes for the Lord's Supper, and shared their meals with great joy and generosity. (Acts 2:44–46)

The Trappings of Name-Brand Tennis Shoes

Pricey shoe-wearing preachers have come under scrutiny in the past few years. And honestly, we can't blame society for raising an eyebrow at pastors wearing $500 shoes and boarding private jets for exotic monthlong "sabbaticals." (But also, how does one acquire a luxurious plane to a tropical destination? Asking for a friend.)

But do you know what you don't see among trending topics? Pastors who barely make it paycheck to paycheck yet faithfully tithe. Pastors who, without hesitation, swing by the grocery store to purchase groceries for a widow down to her last can of beans. Pastors who rush to the side of grieving families at 2:00 a.m. shortly after hearing unfathomable news no parent should ever have to bear alone. These pastors live what they preach and quietly serve under the radar. Sadly, the fame and fortune–seeking "pastors" (we use this term loosely since these types are not shepherds but wolves among the flock) taint the reputation of the good ones.

We married a few of those good ones and have seen them serve for minimal to moderate compensation . . . and, at times, for nothing. Unfortunately, the fancy-shoed wolves and justified fear of turning evil due to an overfondness for money have made churchgoers skeptical of servants of the Lord owning nice things or taking a hiatus. Jessica nearly boils over every time she hears smart comments about Jonathan's clothing or their family vacations.

We must be paying you too much. Your husband can wear all those name-brand things.

Oh wow, you went on vacation there*? I wish I could afford to travel like that!*

The comments might be made in jest, but the speakers don't realize that he snagged those name-brand shoes from Facebook Marketplace, eBay, or Goodwill. Or that their family vacation only transpired because of someone's generosity. What other job attracts this much skepticism or criticism in reference to financial choices? Assumptions are rarely accurate and, in this case, are even utterly erroneous.

We would dare to say that most pastors aren't living the high life in immaculate mansions and hanging with their boy Justin Bieber on the weekends. And many ride the line of poverty with zero health insurance while serving the church more than full-time. Let's get real: Are any pastors not on call 24/7? Even bi-vocational ones aren't genuinely part-time. They serve beyond full-time for part-time pay, and technically, according to Scripture, it shouldn't be this way:

> Elders who do their work well should be respected and paid well, especially those who work hard at both preaching and teaching. For the Scripture says, "You must not muzzle an ox to keep it from eating as it treads out the grain." And in another place, "Those who work deserve their pay!" (1 Tim. 5:17–18)

For the pastor's wife or pastor forced to explain financial decisions to church members—*and social media constituents*—we understand your exhaustion and frustration from continually feeling pressured to clarify how you spend your money. Take heart in knowing not every questioning church member is criticizing your financial choices. Some are genuinely curious. A few might be critical—and to those who are, you owe no explanation. You don't have to allow anger and bitterness a seat at your emotional table. You can smile, shake your head, and move on. Feel what you feel and then remind yourself you aren't doing any of this for affirmation. You do this for God alone.

The "innocent" questions won't sting as much when you guard your heart against sinking into the rising sea of anger. Only trouble comes from bitterness: "Look after each other so that none of you fails to receive the grace of God. Watch out that no poisonous root of bitterness grows up to trouble you, corrupting many" (Heb. 12:15).

Flat-Earth Logic

People know what they see. If they can't see it, some question it. Take, for example, flat-earthers. Did you know a whole group still believes planet Earth is flat? They are convinced the explorations of space, including Armstrong's first steps on the moon, are all a hoax. Stephanie met a flat-earther one day and listened to his logic. No argument could deter him from his belief. No amount of reasoning could alter his credence. He couldn't see a round Earth from his vantage point and was set on discrediting it.

Is it wrong to question popular narratives? We don't think so. We should study and seek and never settle for human words alone. What does God say? What does His Word teach us? What evidence is laid out for us? We live by faith, but God's Word is also saturated with evidence.

Before we can stray too far off-topic, we'll get to our point: people in our churches and communities see their local pastors mainly on Sundays (and Wednesdays for those who still meet midweekly). They have no idea what pastors do during the rest of the week. A young, curious adult recently asked Stephanie's husband, Isaac, what job he did during the week. Isaac chuckled and patiently answered. This guy was shocked to discover Isaac spent time in his office at the church *not on a Sunday*. He was innocently inquisitive. But some aren't as innocent in their observations.

"What do you and your husband do every day?" Jessica cringes every time she's asked this. Do people imagine the two of them are sipping margs and smoking cigars on their front-porch rockers all day, or what? This question triggers her because, too often, she can barely catch her breath on her roller-coaster-ride life. In her bone-tired state, she has to catch herself before ripping off unsuspecting heads because her trauma from past church hurt has turned this question into "fighting words."

Despite her flesh's inclination to throat punch somebody, Jessica has learned to laugh it off and gently explain what they do (if the person is not snarky or accusatory when they ask). In those rare moments when a prickly individual gets nosy, she doesn't defend herself because she doesn't owe an explanation. Those who serve faithfully in the church know what they do outside church services. And that is enough.

If you are the recipient of probing questions and feel as though you could explode from the snide remarks thinly disguised as curiosity, we see you. We know how tirelessly you give of your time and emotions. And God sees too. Don't let someone's petulant behavior deter your joy. Be angry momentarily, and then release your anger to the One who can handle it. The wise remain calm: "A fool is quick-tempered, but a wise person stays calm when insulted" (Prov. 12:16).

Ministry life can be vexing, like an impatient preschooler tugging at Mom's jogger pants for the umpteenth time while droning on and on in agony over the torture of being dragged through the aisles of Target. (Why children don't appreciate a place where you can simultaneously sip a steaming latte, purchase milk, and discover a blanket that must have been knit by angels boggles our minds.) But just as a mother loves said preschooler despite the lack of appreciation for the Disney World of all shops, ministry leaders can choose to love those who misunderstand them, get blinded by tradition, or allow money to distort their rationale. After all, we are also flawed humans serving imperfect people for the sake of our perfect God. And no amount of irritation should ever dissuade our service.

14

The Pastor's Wife
Dances Too

There are shortcuts to happiness, and dancing is one of them.

—Unknown

As most of us know, the everyday responsibilities of running a home can be exhausting (even for us moms on "school breaks"). Having fun becomes more of a dream when you have other things calling for your attention. Stephanie felt the weight of the busyness on a recent spring break. After a full day of helping one child deep clean and organize their room, Stephanie envisioned the covers calling her name. But then her other two children began craving attention too. Since she knew the week's responsibilities would take her away from home often, she chose her kids over the bed.

Her oldest child had received a game for Christmas that hadn't been touched yet, so they decided to give it a whirl.

Roughly two minutes into their fun, Stephanie was sure this game had been concocted by a group of eight-to-twelve-year-old boys. There was no shortage of scatological sayings and absurd scenarios. Before long, all of them—Stephanie, Isaac, and their three children—were cackling and howling so force-fully, it's a wonder they didn't pee their pants while reading off lines like, "peeing on my poopy."

When Stephanie was a child, you didn't say words like *poop*, *butt*, or any expressions best left in the bathroom (literally). And although she finds her kids hilarious when they guffaw over their bathroom-humor theatrics, she ends up shushing her children when other people might overhear their shenanigans. As a pastor's wife (and churchgoer since the mid-80s), she has always been cautious of expressing too much silliness or utter-ing anything too unseemly. She still cringes when church people gawk at her children as they chortle over bodily gases. And this hesitancy bleeds over into her actions. What is appropriate and what is entirely inappropriate for a person serving in the min-istry? Are we free to express ourselves like everyone else can?

Why Quirky Pastors' Wives Are the Coolest

Jessica has wrestled with this same question throughout her years in ministry. If she could pull a *Back to the Future* move and time-travel to visit her young-twenties self, she would have so much to tell her. (You know, unless the universe would im-plode from two Jessicas existing in one moment together. That could put a damper on the whole experience.) She would grab her young self by her tense, questioning shoulders and assure her she was not required to become a replica of the pastors' wives she grew up seeing. There was nothing wrong with the women she observed as a child and adolescent, but she was nothing like them. She was unique. It was okay, extraordinary even, not to be them. She could be herself, goofy and all, and she didn't have to fit the mold of Mrs. PPPW. Being a pastor's wife meant walking alongside Jonathan in ministry while utilizing the strengths and personality God entrusted to her. Nothing else mattered.

Jessica would have been much more at ease in her skin if she had known this truth in her twenties. We all would have. We pray we can pave the way for more church leaders to embrace the strength of their quirkiness and distinctive personalities. God desires to use the idiosyncrasies He created in us for His glory. Why would we attempt to live the opposite of how He created us? We were made and chosen by God and for Him.

> But you are not like that, for you are a chosen people. You are royal priests, a holy nation, God's very own possession. As a result, you can show others the goodness of God, for he called you out of the darkness into his wonderful light. (1 Pet. 2:9)

God's joy flows through us to others when we embrace how we were designed.

> You made me; you created me.
>   Now give me the sense to follow your commands.
> May all who fear you find in me a cause for joy,
>   for I have put my hope in your word. (Ps. 119:73–74)

Recently when Jessica attended a staff meeting at church, one of the leaders spoke over Jessica words of affirmation that fell on her spirit like a healing salve: "Thank you for being real. And for being funny and goofy and not feeling like you have to act a certain way. It breaks down walls and helps us know you're not perfect." This acknowledgment and acceptance of her uniqueness meant the world to her.

Jessica is feisty. You know she loves you when you become the recipient of a butt-slap. When her arm winds up, and she whacks full throttle directly on your behind, you have made it into the friend club. We're sure our prairie-living pastor-wife ancestors from the 1800s roll over in their graves at every butt-slapping, but that's Jessica.

When she began working in a youth group at a young age, she and a good friend would whack each other on the butt to see who could leave the deepest, reddest hand imprint on each other's back ends. The teen girls thought it was hilarious, so they began exchanging butt-whacks too. They would howl until the tears poured down their cheeks and their abs were as sore as if they'd completed an intense core workout. These former teens still remember those days and chortle at the memory. Jessica built relationships through laughter. The silliness led to the girls being comfortable with her. They opened up to her because they knew she was real. She would love them rather than judge them through whatever mistakes they made. She listened to them and guided them in her unique, intriguing way.

Laughter brings us together. When you discover joy with others despite the chaos of the surrounding world and burst out in laughter, even in inopportune times, you can connect emotionally, mentally, and spiritually. When you embrace your personality and accept others for theirs, God's creativity is fully displayed. If you're a book nerd who meanders down the aisles of bookstores breathing in the scent of crisp pages, embrace it and invite someone to join you as you scan those colorful stacks. If you binge crime shows in your free time, invite a church acquaintance to a popcorn and true crime night. If adventuring is your jam, join women from your small group for a hiking and sightseeing outing. Whatever you love, invite people in on your fun.

We allow stigmas and stereotypes to blind us to God's purpose in our eccentricities and individuality when we shouldn't.

When our idea of what a church leader is runs off-track, we manufacture a dull and lifeless image of Jesus. And He is anything but. Before we ever existed, He knew fun and fellowship and created us in His multifaceted, innovative image. We are meant to reflect our Potter's creative genius: "Yet you, Lord, are our Father. We are the clay, you are the potter; we are all the work of your hand" (Isa. 64:8 NIV). He created us with differences for a purpose. When we conceal our God-woven personas or try to become someone we're not, the people we serve miss out on the intricate beauty of who God is.

Free to Dance

We weren't there, but we're pretty sure Jessica popped out of her mother's womb dancing. She danced in her bedroom, with her friends, and everywhere she went. She even choreographed dance routines and proudly performed them in front of her parents, who were gracious enough to patiently watch every one. To create and feel the passion behind the music was a welcome release for her.

When Jessica became an adult, she wasn't sure where dancing fit, if it even fit at all. She decided she wouldn't dance in public unless *public* meant a sea of strangers on a cruise ship in the middle of the ocean. Then she'd dance the night away with her husband. But she avoided it otherwise, which was not easy. Dancing was a part of her, just as it is a part of so many of us. (Not that we all are born with rhythm. Just ask Stephanie.)

In her thirties, Jessica found the freedom to dance again when God brought friends into her life who related to her. They had allowed a *Footloose* town type of influence to freeze their dancing shoes, but they found their freedom again together. They questioned the narrative that dancing is a sin not to be indulged in by Christians, especially pastors' wives.

"Prim and proper" was the cultural depiction of women in ministry, and she had gotten distracted by this falsity. Fear of the church's rejection or of our husbands being reprimanded can rule our actions rather than the truth of what God's Word teaches us.

Jessica started dancing in celebration at weddings again. She whirled and swayed and bobbed her head on girls' nights. She expressed her joy through dance, and people noticed. Her dancing has given other people the freedom to be themselves and express their joy at these celebrations too.

According to Ecclesiastes, there is a time to wear our dancing shoes. We're given "a time to cry and a time to laugh. A time to grieve and a time to dance" (Eccl. 3:4). Throughout Scripture, dance correlates with praise: "Praise his name with dancing, accompanied by tambourine and harp. For the LORD delights in his people; he crowns the humble with victory" (Ps. 149:3–4). And we know that it can also be an expression of joy, like the Bible describes in Jeremiah: "I will rebuild you, my virgin Israel. You will again be happy and dance merrily with your tambourines" (31:4).

Who invented the lie that Christ-followers shouldn't dance? King David danced. God's people worshiped in dance. And nations from every corner of the earth have expressed themselves through dance since the beginning of time. Dance is a strategic part of God's creation. Who are we to think we can do away with what the God of the universe has designed? This negativity toward letting loose in dance is not new. One of David's wives is the perfect example:

> And David danced before the LORD with all his might, wearing a priestly garment. So David and all the people of Israel brought up the Ark of the Lord with shouts of joy and the blowing of rams' horns.

But as the Ark of the LORD entered the City of David, Michal, the daughter of Saul, looked down from her window. When she saw King David leaping and dancing before the LORD, she was filled with contempt for him. . . . When David returned home to bless his own family, Michal, the daughter of Saul, came out to meet him. She said in disgust, "How distinguished the king of Israel looked today, shamelessly exposing himself to the servant girls like any vulgar person might do!"

David retorted to Michal, "I was dancing before the LORD, who chose me above your father and all his family! He appointed me as the leader of Israel, the people of the Lord, so I celebrate before the Lord." (2 Sam. 6:14–16, 20–21)

Some people will criticize you for dancing for joy because their preferences have clouded their judgment. But if David didn't stop dancing when his wife reprimanded him, then why should we?

Free to Worship

Jenna grew up in a traditional church where "worship" consisted of familiar hymns and praise tunes sung in reverent tones without a hint of movement. Arms were crossed, not raised to heaven in adoration. Hand clapping? Is this a ball game or a church service? Jenna knew nothing outside of this orthodox box. She never questioned the habitual routine until she visited the church where her boyfriend (now husband) led worship for a youth group. The lights danced across the room as the worship leaders praised their friend Jesus and led the teens into His presence. There she froze, awestruck by the sincerity with which people worshiped God unashamedly. This type of worship fascinated her. People lifted holy hands, danced before the Lord, and entered the throne room of God as a unit. Worship brought unity while simultaneously ushering individuals to Jesus's feet. It changed the way Jenna viewed church and made her crave genuinely expressive forms of worship.

Jenna would love to shake a few Christians awake who are stuck in the same old, same old. Some church people have failed to show the world what true joy is through worshiping their King. They sleepily perch in the same pew they've metaphorically snored in weekly for years, barely peeking out from their eyelids when the Holy Spirit stirs.

How do we expect to reach the world in a dead church? How can we teach our children that following Jesus and getting involved with the local church body is life-giving when our "worship" lulls us into complacency? How can we intrigue curious visitors to worship with us when we go through the motions void of feeling?

Worshiping Jesus is intoxicating. Serving in the local church brings unmatched satisfaction and joy. This is the message that we should live inside and outside the church's walls. But we don't always get it right. Too many churches are chained to what used to be rather than walking in the freedom of what is because of Christ. He is alive and active. Aren't we supposed to imitate Him? His Word paints a vivid picture of vibrant praise: "Come, everyone! Clap your hands! Shout to God with joyful praise!" (Ps. 47:1). "Come, let us sing to the LORD! Let us shout joyfully to the Rock of our salvation" (95:1).

Free to Have Fun

One of Stephanie's closest friends growing up was a PK. This friendship gave Stephanie a ringside view of the complexities of a pastor's family. Her friend's mother was a vocal, decisive leader with charisma unseen in most pastors' wives in their strict, legalistic circle of churches. Most slipped into the background so their husbands could remain in the spotlight. Heaven forbid a pastor's wife have opinions outside her husband's or embody any trait that could turn into a "spectacle." But this pastor's wife always appeared to be unapologetically herself. She supported her husband, but she didn't hide behind the distorted view of meekness her denomination clung to. To be meek is to be in control of your strength. But in these people's eyes, you showed your meekness by shutting your mouth and following your husband's whims without contradiction.

Stephanie recalls her friend whispering that her mom had taken her to her favorite country music vocalist's concert. Since the churches they associated with were led by men who spat and hollered from their pulpits about the evils of CCM (contemporary Christian music), attending any secular concert was a no-go. Despite the "rules," this mom raised her children to love God *and* good music. And she left a mark on Stephanie. Christians, pastors' wives, and leaders in the church were not obligated to fit the cookie-cutter mold. They could laugh and enjoy life while serving Jesus. Being bland wasn't a requirement.

Somewhere along the way, we've exchanged the truth of God's Word for our interpretation based on the culture surrounding us. But creating rules to run from style, trends, and fun within our culture doesn't make us more spiritual; it makes us Pharisees. The proof is in Matthew:

> Then Jesus said to the crowds and to his disciples, "The teachers of religious law and the Pharisees are the official interpreters of the law of Moses. So practice and obey whatever they tell you, but don't follow their example. For they don't practice what they teach. They crush people with unbearable religious demands and never lift a finger to ease the burden. Everything they do is for show." (23:1–5)

Shows are for the theater. Our lives aren't for viewers' consumption, entertainment, or gossip. We shine the light of Jesus in the way He created us to shine. Looking like the ministry leader or churchgoer beside us is not shining the light. It's hiding from the light—creating a false persona rather than standing in God's unique creativity. Don't quit dancing. Don't stop inviting people to join you in a life of zest and vitality. Don't dim your light to match the dullness others have invented. And by golly, laugh at the poopy fart jokes. You know they're hilarious.

15

The Pastor's Wife
Has Her Own Callings Too

> When God calls you to do something, He provides everything
> it takes to get it done.
>
> —Nancy DeMoss Wolgemuth

In the spring of 2022, we led our first multiday retreat for pastors' wives. The hostess of this weekend event had secured a gorgeous house on the bank of Lake Wylie. Our jaws dropped as we toured what felt like a mansion to us. We had never stayed somewhere so pristine . . . and so white. From the white walls to the white furniture, we were a tad intimidated. Our coffee-stained furniture, worn from years of withstanding the antics of small children, was no match to this house, where the furniture looked fresh out of the pages of Joanna Gaines's *Magnolia Journal*. It wouldn't surprise us one iota if Joanna and the owner of this lake house had braided each other's hair in middle school and now exchanged paint samples and fabric swatches on weekends spent sipping fruity drink concoctions at the lake house together.

Over our glamorous weekend at this "mansion," we bonded with a group of ladies we'll never forget. We were diverse in age, personality, and denomination, but we had one thing in common: we had devoted our lives to the church and were all bone-tired from our years of service, whether two or twenty-plus. (#Ain'tNoTiredLikeChurchMinistryTired.) Most of us were pastors' wives, but some were pastors, and one worship pastor's story left a mark on us all.

This woman's husband was originally the one in pastoral ministry, but circumstances shifted, upending the position he held. God removed them from the church where her husband served as the youth minister, which left them at a proverbial crossroads. As they sought God's leading, He guided them to a church needing a worship pastor. Our new retreat friend's husband did something almost unheard of in church circles. His eyes opened wide to his wife's gifted vocals and her heart for worship, and he encouraged her to apply for the worship pastor position at this church. She was hesitant because this was not part of the plan. They were looking for a role for *him*, not her. But as she laid down her insecurity and surrendered her dreams to whatever God had in store for them, she took a leap of faith and applied. To her surprise, she got the job. Her husband supported her and took a backseat, serving as a volunteer wherever they needed him. Eventually, another place on the church's staff opened, and our friend's husband became the next youth pastor of their church—their story brought full circle.

Called in a Man's World

In a world where men are usually viewed as the "called ones," God used a guy full of humility to remind us of an important truth that weekend. Women are called too. God has plans for His daughters, just like He does for His sons. What would have been the outcome for our friend's husband had he ignored his wife's calling? Her calling intimately intertwined with his, and ultimately, her calling led to his being fulfilled.

Not everyone's story is identical to this couple's, but God has His own plans for us too. Remember the woman at the well? She met Jesus face-to-face and was radically changed. In turn, a host of Samaritans came to know Jesus because she spoke up and shared her testimony with her city:

> Many Samaritans from the village believed in Jesus because the woman had said, "He told me everything I ever did!" When they came out to see him, they begged him to stay in their village. So he stayed for two days, long enough for many more to hear his message and believe. (John 4:39–41)

Lives are eternally impacted when we get bold—when we quit concealing our stories and talents behind the guise of being a good wife and mom. Of course, these titles are essential. But other callings are no less crucial because of them. There's no telling who will miss out on the goodness of God if we bury our callings beneath our husbands' shadows and our insecurities.

Jessica began following God at a young age. She was a bit of a romantic growing up, so it was no surprise when she felt called to missions in the eighth grade. (Read her journals to get a front-row seat to her bleeding heart and tortured soul. Who knew twelve-year-olds could feel such *big* feelings?) She had no idea how this calling would pan out, but she would build a hut in the jungles of Africa with her bare hands if God asked her to do so. As a middle schooler, she never could have imagined how God would use her willingness to go.

Upon completing high school, Jessica chose a college and began working toward a degree. We grew up in a time when going to college was what everyone did. We didn't realize there was any other option. It was a given that we'd acquire thousands of dollars in loans to earn a piece of paper that would collect dust, only to discover later on that we didn't want to be a nurse or teacher or whatever we had dedicated four stinking years of our lives learning to do.

Jessica earned a degree and sat on her calling for years before it came to fruition. But her hunger for missions never wavered. Finally, in March 2009, Jessica led her first team to Rwanda. There, she met a pastor in Kigali whose life and ministry would forever connect to hers. To this day, Pastor Jean Baptiste Tushimeyere remains one of the most influential mentors of her life. Jessica's insatiable desire to be with her Rwandan family kept her returning with teams regularly. In 2012, Jean asked Jessica if she would be willing to pray about founding a mission organization where they could officially partner, providing ministry opportunities for people worldwide to go and make disciples.

Jessica was no longer that innocent middle schooler ready to attack the African bush with nothing but her bare hands and intuition. By this time, ministry life had pummeled her resolve and left her and Jonathan in shambles. And the more Jessica strove to serve the people of Rwanda, the more her unhealthy pastor at the time fought against her efforts.

God's deepest, most extravagant calling came during the darkest time in her life and faith journey, so she ran from it for a year and a half. She fed herself lies: *I'm not good enough. I don't have the time because youth ministry is draining enough. So many people would be better at this than me. Many other massive mission organizations are doing so much more than I can do.* Excuses ran her decisions, until one life-giving Sunday service in the fall of 2014.

Jessica and her hubby floundered without a church home after he was wrongly fired. They were jaded and loathed even the thought of serving the church. But one Sunday, they called up a few friends who were churchless and weary too, and together they visited a church where each of them would eventually find healing. During this service, Jessica heard the Lord's voice calling her to quit running from her call to missions. The time had come to pick up the broken pieces and rebuild.

During the worship segment of the service, the worship leaders led the congregation in an old Jesus Culture song, "Come Away." This song had long been Jessica's favorite tune, and it would eventually inspire her nonprofit's name. Tears trickled down her cheeks as the song's message washed away her insecurities and anger.

When the pastor preached, she knew God was using him to speak directly to her. The pastor claimed there were people present who had yet to move forward in the callings God had placed on their lives, and they needed to speak those callings out loud. When you announce your calling aloud in the presence of your brothers and sisters in Christ, there is no going back. You receive a spiritual covering of accountability and unmatched strength.

That fateful morning is when Jessica truly realized the old saying is true: "Delayed obedience is still disobedience." She'd run from God's calling because she believed He got it wrong. She couldn't be the right one for this crucial mission. But when we study God's Word, we repeatedly find that people who are entirely wrong for the job are the ones God loves to use. Rahab the prostitute who saved the Hebrew spies, Esther the Jewish orphan girl turned Persian queen, and Mary the simple teenage girl and mother of Jesus are all women who were quite ordinary before God called them to their extraordinary tasks. Obedience is the one trait these women shared, and it's the one thing God requires of us. That's it. Jesus fills our weak spots with strength, stability, and steady perseverance. He makes the impossible possible and draws people to Himself through our weaknesses.

The pastor then offered the microphone in front of their large congregation and demanded that *Jessica Lynn Taylor* get off her hind end and come to the front. Or maybe that naming part was the whisper of the Holy Spirit. Either way, Jessica was irresistibly drawn to the altar of an unfamiliar church and boldly planted her feet on the stage. As she shared her call with this brand-new church family, the people in the sound booth flashed her words across the screen. She stared misty-eyed at her calling clearly and tangibly written on the wall while two strong emotions clashed inside her. She felt immense fear but also sensed peace beyond understanding, wrapping her up like a toasty, warm, weighted blanket fresh out of the dryer. God was with her, and the journey of Come Away Missions began in that place.

For the one who has run from your calling, whether out of insecurity or from believing you'll get in your husband's way, stop limiting God. He is fully capable of using whomever He wants, whenever He chooses. Your gender and your husband's call do not negate your calling.

Like Jessica, perhaps you've dipped your toes into shallow waters where you feel safe. Maybe you've scratched the surface of your calling, as she did when she took those early mission trips. But God is calling you to dive headfirst into the deep, murky waters where your physical eyes close and your spiritual eyes open wide.

The Great Commission was not a suggestion: "And then he told them, 'Go into all the world and preach the Good News to everyone'" (Mark 16:15). *You have a responsibility.* "Let each one live his life in the situation the Lord assigned when God called him. This is what I command in all the churches" (1 Cor.

7:17 CSB). As you step into the call, you'll traverse wild, unrestrained waves and slosh relentlessly to and fro with nothing but the presence of the Holy Spirit. His peace will sustain you, and you'll finally break free from the box in which you enclosed yourself.

How to Get Unstuck

Watching a toddler dress is entertaining. As they grunt and huff, jamming a foot into an armhole or cramming their head into a sleeve, it takes everything in you to hold yourself together. You know how easy it would be to dress this stubborn kiddo, but you allow them to exercise their independence. The entire dressing experience would take only 5.3 seconds (give or take) if they'd pay attention to which body part belonged in which hole. But toddlers, like their parents, tend to complicate simple tasks. We all have been guilty of overcomplicating what should be simple.

Jenna relates to this overzealous toddler. (Not that she can't dress herself; she's got that down to a science.) As an adolescent and even a full-grown adult, she didn't know what she wanted to be when she grew up. She had no eighth grade, fire-coming-down-from-heaven type of call. Like Jessica, she attended college because it was what everyone did. When it came time to choose a major, Jenna flipped through the college catalog and might as well have blindly shoved her pointer finger onto a random page and called it a day. She had zero plans for using her health science degree, but it would be an excellent notch in her belt, and maybe she would figure out how to use it later. But years passed, and even after her thirtieth birthday, she was still clueless about what she wanted to do.

Jenna's husband knew what God wanted him to do. He was so sure of his calling, while Jenna felt lost. She craved one of those lightning bolt moments, like when God shot water-lapping fire straight down from heaven because the prophet Elijah said, "Pretty please." And a precise road map would have been fabulous too. But He chose to speak a little less boisterously to her. We forget that God doesn't always speak in a whirlwind or through a burning bush. He also whispers in a still, small voice.

We discussed possibly starting a fun little pastors' wives podcast three years before writing this book. We had no idea how God would grow this idea into a worldwide ministry. After several months of God multiplying the reach of our "hobby," a light bulb switched on for Jenna. Ian led a worship nonprofit where he pastored other pastors, pouring into them, praying for them, and worshiping with them. Now Jenna was ministering to pastors' wives in the same manner. She pastored other pastors' wives. It still floors her to think about all God has done and continues to do through a girl filled with insecurities and questions. But this revelation of her purpose and talents didn't end there.

As we mentioned previously, Jenna has been a photographer for years. She was already using her gift in the church, but God stretched her again in the summer of 2022. Behind the scenes, she had been serving Jessica's nonprofit, Come Away Missions, for a few years. But every year, when Jessica would ask her to come to Rwanda to document God's movement through her photography, she never felt the time was right.

As she had done many times, Jessica casually asked if Jenna would make the trip to Rwanda with her summer 2022 team. Without pause, Jenna answered, "Yes!" You could have knocked Jessica over with a single strand of hair from the shock. Jenna's life would never be the same after spending time with these people and capturing their warmth and joy through the lens of her camera. She wept as she witnessed firsthand how God could use simple obedience.

Through serving on the creative team in her church and taking pictures for Come Away Missions, Jenna realized God had called her to capture what He was doing. Photography was no longer her business; it was her ministry. God had called her, and her calling was as important as her husband's.

Sometimes we get tunnel vision, like toddlers dressing themselves. We overcomplicate God's calling and overlook the gifts staring us in the face. We push and shove to fit anywhere other than the obvious, a square peg looking for a round hole. Don't underestimate what God can do with a willing heart and simple talents, no matter how small. He uses everything and wastes nothing. We need to get busy.

> Just as each one has received a gift, use it to serve others, as good stewards of the varied grace of God. If anyone speaks, let it be as one who speaks God's words; if anyone serves, let it be from the strength God provides, so that God may be glorified through Jesus Christ in everything. To him be the glory and the power forever and ever. Amen. (1 Pet. 4:10–11 CSB)

Don't Rush the Process

In a crowded stadium in Pensacola, Florida, Stephanie weaved through a sea of women while awkwardly attempting to avoid a baby bump collision. She and a group of ladies from her church were attending a women's conference where various female authors and speakers shared tear-inducing testimonies and passionate sermons while the audience sniffled and nodded their heads in solidarity. As she listened to each story and soaked in every detail, a spark ignited within her. A vision of herself writing and encouraging women as these authors were doing on stage slipped into her mind.

Stephanie didn't write; at least, she hadn't recently. As English majors do, she had written plenty of papers in college, but her writing post-college consisted of a few pitiful poems and one or two devotionals no one had seen. But here she dreamed, picturing herself as an author. It made zero sense. Her writing, especially creative writing, was subpar at best.

Despite a million questions and a thousand insecurities, Stephanie started a blog shortly after her third child was born. Years of frustration and on again, off again blogging followed, and the vision Stephanie had experienced faded into a giant question mark. What was she doing with her life? Were her words making any difference? It would take nearly a decade, a big move, and two new friends for her vision to come to fruition. Instead of a stage, God would give her a podcast mic to use to speak to the hearts of thousands of women. And instead of writing a book alone, here she sits, pecking away at keys and formulating words alongside her two best friends. This calling was never hers alone, but it took root long before it would be fulfilled.

When God is kind enough to give us a glimpse into the future, He's not always intending for us to make it happen *now*. Sometimes we have spiritual growth and maturing to face before we see the results of our calling. Stephanie sure did. With obedience came a slow, arduous process of God gradually winnowing away the chaff in her life. Disheartened by her lack of forward movement, she would remind herself of her vision and trust in God's timing. Through doubting came stronger faith. Through questioning came perseverance. And ultimately, through the waiting came purpose.

You are called whether you are a pastor's wife, a church leader, or simply a member of the body of Christ. What you consider small, God deems significant. Don't believe us? Just imagine the most mansion-like lake house you ever did see and ask those alabaster white walls what they witnessed on our first overnight retreat. They'll tell you what God can do with a reluctant but willing woman ready to bury the excuses and step into her God-sized dreaming shoes. And He can do the same with you!

Conclusion

Few things in life are better than a road trip with your besties, or at least this is true for the three of us. To say we are bougie travel buddies would be an understatement. There are never enough cup holders for all our drinks and barely adequate space to contain our heaps of luggage. Don't even think about telling us we don't *need* our brown sugar shaken espressos, peppermint white mocha lattes, forty-ounce travel cups for H_2O hydration, and Dr Pepper Strawberries & Cream Zeros. And don't you dare suggest we bypass our blessed snacks of beef jerky, organic gummy bears, or boiled peanuts. Priorities, people. Once we settle in with our bounty of sustenance, we crank up our Spotify playlists and dance like eighth graders who sneaked into the high school prom. Jenna recently discovered a nightlight contraption we can plug into the car adapter that dances lights across the ceiling. It's a whole vibe. Like we said—bougie.

We might love road trips, but none of us enjoy the driving part. So we take turns being the responsible adult behind the wheel while the other two act like children. We all have distinctive driving techniques and idiosyncrasies while navigating unfamiliar highways. Jessica is the least anxious of the bunch and finds the thought of being stranded without gas on the side of the road thrilling—a true adventure—while Jenna and Stephanie would vomit at the thought of running out of gas on their watch. Jenna needs to feel in complete control behind the wheel. She pays close attention to the GPS and mentally prepares for each turn. Jessica is the thoughtful sort of friend who snags the GPS out of Jenna's view, forcing her to relinquish control . . . but Jenna never fully raises her white flag.

"Where is the next turn? Do I need to be in the right lane or left? What does 'get into the left lane in a little bit' mean? On a scale of a ninety-degree burning-rubber-on-two-tires immediate turn to a leisurely lane swap within the next mile, exactly how little are we talking? Yes, I do need to know! No, I am not okay."

Even when her best friend plans to take them safely to their destination (potential detours included), Jenna still wants all the information up front. The thought of missing a turn or unwittingly entering a toll road void of exits, destining them to an extortionate, unplanned bill and sending them all into a panic would be devastating. (Not that we would know! All hypothetical, of course. #TrueStory.)

Jenna trusts Jessica with her life. If there were a zombie apocalypse, Jenna would cling to Jessica's shirttail with confidence that Jessica would flat eat a zombie alive before it could touch her. But behind the wheel, Jenna's faith in her zombie-slaying friend wavers.

Isn't this like Christians? We have entrusted our entire lives to the God of the universe, but we still insist on viewing the "GPS." Sure, God sees the whole map and will 100 percent keep us on course, only detouring when necessary. But we think we need to know the when and the why; if we don't, we freeze.

We have turned the will of God into a mystery. And like detectives, we search for clues to answers we can't yet handle

. . . as if we learned nothing from Eve eating that knowledge-bestowing fruit. (Spoiler alert: worst decision *ever*. Literally.)

In our ministries, we have taken a multitude of detours. We've clung to Jesus and badgered Him with a thousand questions (which He patiently endures). We've worried, panicked, questioned, and wept a gallon of tears, but God steadily guides us, one turn on the GPS at a time. Destination after destination, He has proven He is a five-star navigator. Through both toxic and healthy churches and pastors, we have been hurt but have grown. We couldn't see why these detours popped up, but God's providence actively directed us to the churches and ministries we get to serve in now. Nothing is by happenstance. Nothing is meaningless.

Friend, God has planned out every detail, and He knows all the answers while resting in your passenger seat, waiting for you to listen and follow His directions. He's not forcefully taking the wheel but is asking you to go where He has called you.

Whether we married a pastor, are a pastor, or serve in the body of Christ, we are all called. Short, tall, tatted-up, pearl-loving, on stage or behind the scenes, we are loved, chosen, and, because of Christ, made worthy of that calling. Matthew 28:19–20 is where our journey starts and ends. God's got the in-between.

> Therefore go and make disciples of all nations, baptizing them in the name of the Father and of the Son and of the Holy Spirit, and teaching them to obey everything I have commanded you. And surely I am with you always, to the very end of the age. (NIV)

Pop some road trip munchies in your mouth, situate your abundance of beverages, and allow God to navigate as you cruise uncharted roadways. Take the detours in stride. And, for goodness' sake, keep your eyes on the road ahead. Trust us; you don't want to miss a thing.

Acknowledgments

When God led us to write this book, He proved to the world that He has a sense of humor. Thank you, Lord, for using three silly, flawed friends to encourage women in the church. Your ability to take something broken and turn it into something worthwhile is not lost on us.

Isaac, Jonathan, and Ian, thank you for being supportive husbands and teammates. You patiently held down the fort for a bazillion late-night brainstorming sessions and weekends when our noses were glued to our laptops. Without you carrying the weight of parenting much of the time, we never would have been able to complete this book. Thank you for keeping us sane(ish) and laughing when we wanted to cry. You are our best friends!

Bryce, Bentley, Avery G., Grace, Oliviya, Addie, and Avery A., you are our favorite little humans on the planet. Without your cuddles and hilarity, we never could have made it through the book-writing process. Thank you for sharing your mommies with a host of strangers. You are world changers, and we are ridiculously blessed to be your moms.

Moms, dads, stepparents, siblings, and extended family, you were our first loves and much of the reason we are who we are today. Thank you for being our supporters from birth. You deserve a million gold medals for dealing with our shenanigans.

To our closest friends (you know who you are), thank you for cheering wholeheartedly with and for us. Squealing with you and pinching each other has made writing a book much sweeter. You are our tribe.

To Summerville Baptist, Village Church, and Church of the Highlands, thank you for your constant support and being the best church families we could ever hope for. You have served us as much as we've helped you, if not more, and we are forever grateful.

Without our podcast listeners, email subscribers, Facebook community group members, and social media friends, we would never have been able to start this project. Thank you for your honest feedback on potential book titles and content. This book is for you, and your love and acceptance of us are humbling.

We could have never begun this project without the help of our sweet mentor and friend, Karen Stiller. Thank you for believing in us and being a rock we could steady ourselves on when we thought our writing could never be good enough. Because of your wisdom, guidance, and editorial skills, we landed our dream agent. You are #PastorWifeyGoals.

To Mary DeMuth, thank you for seeing the potential in three jokesters who live for dance reels. As an agent, you get down in the muck with us and lift us out when we feel we can't form one more word. Thank you for fighting for us and working tirelessly to get our words out into the world. Working with you is a dream.

Baker Books, we pinch ourselves every day at the thought of being one of your authors. Thank you for taking a chance on us and believing in this book's message. Patnacia, you have made us feel like we belong in the Baker family. Thank you for your excitement over this project and for opening the door for us at Baker Books.

To the ones who have taken the time to hear our hearts on these pages, thank you for purchasing our book. If you're reading these acknowledgments, you are our people. Thank you for listening. We hope your burdens feel lighter and your abs are tighter from all the belly laughs. You are incredible!

Notes

Chapter 3 The Pastor's Wife Curses (or Inserts Foot in Mouth) Too

1. University of Rochester Medical Center, "Understanding the Teen Brain," URMC Adult and Children's Health Encyclopedia, accessed August 1, 2023, https://www.urmc.rochester.edu/encyclopedia/content.aspx?Content TypeID=1&ContentID=3051.

Chapter 5 The Pastor's Wife Fights with Her Husband Too

1. Louie Giglio, *Indescribable: 100 Devotions for Kids about God and Science*, illustrated by Nicola Anderson (Nashville: Thomas Nelson, 2017), 14.

Chapter 6 The Pastor's Wife Fakes Headaches Too

1. Sheila Wray Gregoire, Rebecca Gregoire Lindenbach, and Joanna Sawatsky, *The Great Sex Rescue: The Lies You've Been Taught and How to Recover What God Intended* (Grand Rapids: Baker Books, 2021).

2. Sheila Wray Gregoire and Keith Gregoire, *The Good Guy's Guide to Great Sex* (Grand Rapids: Zondervan, 2022); Sheila Wray Gregoire, *The Good Girl's Guide to Great Sex* (Grand Rapids: Zondervan, 2022).

3. "What If Talking to Your Kids about Sex Didn't Need to Be So Awkward?," Bare Marriage, accessed July 27, 2023, https://baremarriage.com/the-whole-story/.

4. "The Porn Phenomenon," Barna, accessed July 27, 2023, https://www.barna.com/the-porn-phenomenon/#.VqZoN_krIdU.

5. James Strong, "G2133: eunoia," *The New Strong's Exhaustive Concordance of the Bible* (Nashville: Thomas Nelson, 1990), 37–38.

6. Warren W. Wiersbe, *The Bible Exposition Commentary: New Testament*, vol. 1 (Colorado Springs: Cook, 1989), 590–91.

AUTHORS

JESSICA TAYLOR, JENNA ALLEN, and **STEPHANIE GILBERT** are the three cohosts of *Pastors' Wives Tell All*, a podcast by pastors' wives for church leaders and anyone desiring to peek inside their proverbial glass houses. From three different churches and denominations, they are breaking down walls within the church and crushing PW stereotypes with a little ministry therapy and a whole lot of Jesus—plus the occasional Instagram dance party!

You can learn more about their ministry at Pastors WivesTellAll.com.

STEPHANIE GILBERT is a blogger, speaker, and youth minister's wife who has made it her life's mission to seek out joy amid the junk of everyday life and lead other women (and teen girls) to passionately thrive in joy-filled lives too. She believes laughter is truly the best medicine and joy flourishes in the hard spaces. Stephanie has had her writing published on reputable sites such as *Scary Mommy* and *Her View From Home*. Get to know her better and be encouraged on Instagram.

Connect with Stephanie:

MsStephanieGilbert.com

f @MsStephanieGilbert

⊙ @MsStephanieGilbert

JESSICA TAYLOR is a speaker, nonprofit owner, and pastor's wife. She is a dynamic leader and creative who runs Come Away Missions and DO GOOD Project, a nonprofit serving the people of Rwanda. She sends multiple teams to Rwanda, Africa, each year and empowers Rwandan artisans by helping them monetize their beautiful creations. Jessica fights for women to see their worth in Christ and to make an impact in the world through their unique giftings and callings.

Connect with Jessica:

ComeAwayMissions.com and DoGoodProject.net

f @ComeAwayMissions and @DoGoodProjectColGa

⊙ @Jessica_Taylor_83 and @Come_Away_Missions and @Do_Good_Project_

JENNA ALLEN is a creative, photographer, tech wiz, speaker, and discipleship/worship pastor's wife. She also specializes in business branding, logos, and web-  site design. Through her perfectionism and keen eye for detail, she brings beauty and a clear message into every project she touches. You can learn more about her business on her website and get to know her more personally on Instagram.

Connect with Jenna:

JennaAllenDesign.com

 @JennaAllenDesign

 @JennaAllen and @JennaAllenDesign